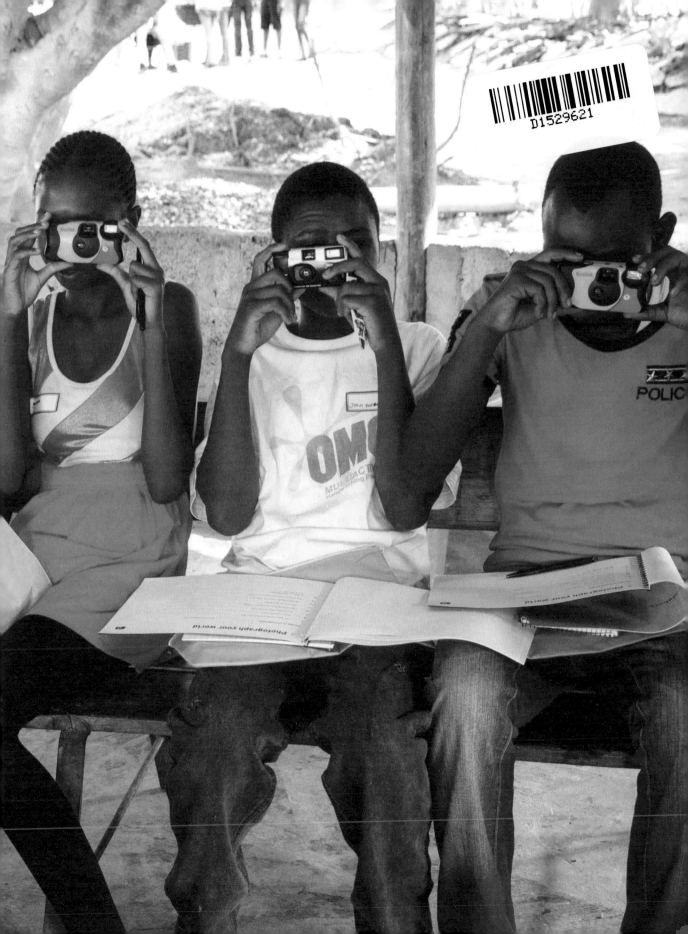

The Field Guide to Human-Centered Design

By IDEO.org

1st Edition © 2015

ISBN: 978-0-9914063-1-9

Printed in Canada

THE
FIELD GUIDE
TO HUMAN–
CENTERED
DESIGN

DESIGN KIT

Contents

What Does It Mean to Be a Human-Centered Designer?

Embracing human-centered design means believing that all problems, even the seemingly intractable ones like poverty, gender equality, and clean water, are solvable. Moreover, it means believing that the people who face those problems every day are the ones who hold the key to their answer. Human-centered design offers problem solvers of any stripe a chance to design with communities, to deeply understand the people they're looking to serve, to dream up scores of ideas, and to create innovative new solutions rooted in people's actual needs.

At IDEO.org and IDEO, we've used human-centered design for decades to create products, services, experiences, and social enterprises that have been adopted and embraced because we've kept people's lives and desires at the core. The social sector is ripe for innovation, and we've seen time and again how our approach has the power to unlock real impact. Being a human-centered designer is about believing that as long as you stay grounded in what you've learned from people, your team can arrive at new solutions that the world needs. And with this Field Guide, you're now armed with the tools needed to bring that belief to life.

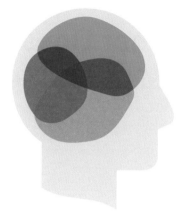

Adopt the Mindsets

Human-centered designers are unlike other problem solvers—we tinker and test, we fail early and often, and we spend a surprising amount of time not knowing the answer to the challenge at hand. And yet, we forge ahead. We're optimists and makers, experimenters and learners, we empathize and iterate, and we look for inspiration in unexpected places. We believe that a solution is out there and that by keeping focused on the people we're designing for and asking the right questions, we'll get there together. We dream up lots of ideas, some that work and some that don't. We make our ideas tangible so that we can test

them, and then we refine them. In the end, our approach amounts to wild creativity, to a ceaseless push to innovate, and a confidence that leads us to solutions we'd never dreamed of when we started. In the Field Guide, we share our philosophy of design and the seven mindsets that set us apart: Empathy, Optimism, Iteration, Creative Confidence, Making, Embracing Ambiguity, and Learning from Failure.

Understand the Process

Human-centered design isn't a perfectly linear process, and each project invariably has its own contours and character. But no matter what kind of design challenge you've got, you'll move through three main phases: Inspiration, Ideation, and Implementation. By taking these three phases in turn, you'll build deep empathy with the communities and individuals you're designing for; you'll figure out how to turn what you've learned into a chance to design a new solution; and you'll build and test your ideas before finally putting them out into the world. At IDEO.org and IDEO, we've used human-centered design to tackle a vast array of design challenges, and though our projects have ranged from social enterprises to communication campaigns to medical devices, this particular approach to creative problem solving has seen us through each time.

INSPIRATION

In this phase, you'll learn how to better understand people. You'll observe their lives, hear their hopes and desires, and get smart on your challenge.

IDEATION

Here you'll make sense of everything that you've heard, generate tons of ideas, identify opportunities for design, and test and refine your solutions.

IMPLEMENTATION

Now is your chance to bring your solution to life. You'll figure out how to get your idea to market and how to maximize its impact in the world.

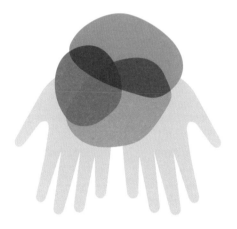

Use the Tools

Though no two human-centered design projects are alike, we draw from the same kit of tools for each of them. For example, to build deep empathy with the people we're trying to serve, we always conduct interviews with them. To maintain creativity and energy, we always work in teams. To keep our thinking generative, sharp, and because it helps us work things through, we always make tangible prototypes of our ideas. And because we rarely get it right the first time, we always share what we've made, and iterate based on the feedback we get. The 57 methods in the Field Guide offer a comprehensive set of exercises and activities that will take you from framing up your design challenge to getting it to market. You'll use some of these methods twice or three times and some not at all as you work through your challenge. But taken as a set, they'll put you on the path to continuous innovation while keeping the community you're designing for squarely at the center of your work.

Trust the Process Even if It Feels Uncomfortable

Human-centered design is a unique approach to problem solving, one that can occasionally feel more like madness than method—but you rarely get to new and innovative solutions if you always know precisely where you're going. The process is designed to get you to learn directly from people, open yourself up to a breadth of creative possibilities, and then zero in on what's most desirable, feasible, and viable for the people you're designing for. You'll find yourself frequently shifting gears through the process, and as you work through its three phases you'll swiftly move from concrete observations to highly abstract thinking, and then right back again into the nuts and bolts of your prototype. We call it diverging and converging. By going really big and broad during the Ideation phase, we dream up all kinds of possible solutions. But because the goal is to have a big impact in the world, we have to then identify what, among that constellation of ideas, has the best shot at really working. You'll diverge and converge a few times, and with each new cycle you'll come closer and closer to a market-ready solution.

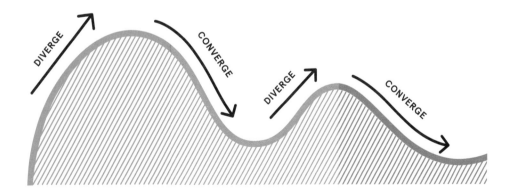

Create Real Impact

Human-centered design is uniquely situated to arrive at solutions that are desirable, feasible, and viable. By starting with humans, their hopes, fears, and needs, we quickly uncover what's most desirable. But that's only one lens through which we look at our solutions. Once we've determined a range of solutions that could appeal to the community we're looking to serve, we then start to home in on what is technically feasible to actually implement and how to make the solution financially viable. It's a balancing act, but one that's absolutely crucial to designing solutions that are successful and sustainable.

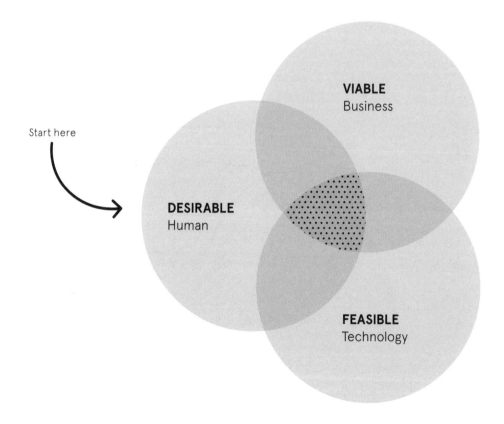

Start here

VIABLE
Business

DESIRABLE
Human

FEASIBLE
Technology

MINDSETS

Creative Confidence

Creative confidence is the notion that you have big ideas, and that you have the ability to act on them.

—David Kelley, Founder, IDEO

Anyone can approach the world like a designer. Often all it takes to unlock that potential as a dynamic problem solver is a bit of creative confidence. Creative confidence is the belief that everyone is creative, and that creativity isn't the capacity to draw or compose or sculpt, but a way of understanding the world.

Creative confidence is the quality that human-centered designers rely on when it comes to making leaps, trusting their intuition, and chasing solutions that they haven't totally figured out yet. It's the belief that you can and will come up with creative solutions to big problems and the confidence that all it takes is rolling up your sleeves and diving in. Creative confidence will drive you to make things, to test them out, to get it wrong, and to keep on rolling, secure in the knowledge that you'll get where you need to go and that you're bound to innovate along the way.

It can take time to build creative confidence, and part of getting there is trusting that the human-centered design process will show you how to bring a creative approach to whatever problem is at hand. As you start with small successes and then build to bigger ones, you'll see your creative confidence grow and before long you'll find yourself in the mindset that you are a wildly creative person.

Make It

You're taking risk out
of the process by making
something simple first.
And you always learn
lessons from it.

—Krista Donaldson, CEO, D-Rev

As human-centered designers, we make because we believe in the power of tangibility. And we know that making an idea real reveals so much that mere theory cannot. When the goal is to get impactful solutions out into the world, you can't live in abstractions. You have to make them real.

Human-centered designers are doers, tinkerers, crafters, and builders. We make using anything at our disposal, from cardboard and scissors to sophisticated digital tools. We build our ideas so that we can test them, and because actually making something reveals opportunities and complexities that we'd never have guessed were there. Making is also a fantastic way to think, and it helps bring into focus the feasibility of our designs. Moreover, making an idea real is an incredibly effective way to share it. And without candid, actionable feedback from people, we won't know how to push our ideas forward.

As you move through the human-centered design process, it doesn't matter what you make, the materials you use, or how beautiful the result is, the goal is always to convey an idea, share it, and learn how to make it better.

Best of all, you can prototype anything at any stage of the process from a service model to a uniform, from a storyboard to the financial details of your solution. As human-centered designers, we have a bias toward action, and that means getting ideas out of our heads and into the hands of the people we're looking to serve.

Learn from Failure

Don't think of it as failure, think of it as designing experiments through which you're going to learn.

—Tim Brown, CEO, IDEO

Failure is an incredibly powerful tool for learning. Designing experiments, prototypes, and interactions and testing them is at the heart of human-centered design. So is an understanding that not all of them are going to work. As we seek to solve big problems, we're bound to fail. But if we adopt the right mindset, we'll inevitably learn something from that failure.

Human-centered design starts from a place of not knowing what the solution to a given design challenge might be. Only by listening, thinking, building, and refining our way to an answer do we get something that will work for the people we're trying to serve. "Fail early to succeed sooner" is a common refrain around IDEO, and part of its power is the permission it gives to get something wrong. By refusing to take risks, some problem solvers actually close themselves off from a real chance to innovate.

Thomas Edison put it well when he said, "I have not failed. I've just found 10,000 ways that won't work." And for human-centered designers, sorting out what won't work is part of finding what will.

Failure is an inherent part of human-centered design because we rarely get it right on our first try. In fact, getting it right on the first try isn't the point at all. The point is to put something out into the world and then use it to keep learning, keep asking, and keep testing. When human-centered designers get it right, it's because they got it wrong first.

Empathy

In order to get to new solutions, you have to get to know different people, different scenarios, different places.

—Emi Kolawole, Editor-in-Residence, Stanford University d.school

---

Empathy is the capacity to step into other people's shoes, to understand their lives, and start to solve problems from their perspectives. Human-centered design is premised on empathy, on the idea that the people you're designing for are your roadmap to innovative solutions. All you have to do is empathize, understand them, and bring them along with you in the design process.

For too long, the international development community has designed solutions to the challenges of poverty without truly empathizing with and understanding the people it's looking to serve. But by putting ourselves in the shoes of the person we're designing for, human-centered designers can start to see the world, and all the opportunities to improve it, through a new and powerful lens.

Immersing yourself in another world not only opens you up to new creative possibilities, but it allows you to leave behind preconceived ideas and outmoded ways of thinking. Empathizing with the people you're designing for is the best route to truly grasping the context and complexities of their lives. But most importantly, it keeps the people you're designing for squarely grounded in the center of your work.

Embrace Ambiguity

We want to give ourselves the permission to explore lots of different possibilities so that the right answer can reveal itself.

—Patrice Martin, Co-Lead and Creative Director, IDEO.org

Human-centered designers always start from the place of not knowing the answer to the problem they're looking to solve. And in a culture that can be too focused on being the first one to the right answer, that's not a particularly comfortable place to be. But by starting at square one, we're forced to get out into the world and talk to the people we're looking to serve. We also get to open up creatively, to pursue lots of different ideas, and to arrive at unexpected solutions. By embracing that ambiguity, and by trusting that the human-centered design process will guide us toward an innovative answer, we actually give ourselves permission to be fantastically creative.

One of the qualities that sets human-centered designers apart is the belief that there will always be more ideas. We don't cling to ideas any longer than we have to because we know that we'll have more. Because human-centered design is such a generative process, and because we work so collaboratively, it's easy to discard bad ideas, hold onto pieces of the so-so ones, and eventually arrive at the good ones.

Though it may seem counterintuitive, the ambiguity of not knowing the answer actually sets up human-centered designers to innovate. If we knew the answer when we started, what could we possibly learn? How could we come up with creative solutions? Where would the people we're designing for guide us? Embracing ambiguity actually frees us to pursue an answer that we can't initially imagine, which puts us on the path to routine innovation and lasting impact.

Optimism

Optimism is the thing that drives you forward.

—John Bielenberg, Founder, Future Partners

We believe that design is inherently optimistic. To take on a big challenge, especially one as large and intractable as poverty, we have to believe that progress is even an option. If we didn't, we wouldn't even try. Optimism is the embrace of possibility, the idea that even if we don't know the answer, that it's out there and that we can find it.

In addition to driving us toward solutions, optimism makes us more creative, encourages us to push on when we hit dead ends, and helps all the stakeholders in a project gel. Approaching problems from the perspective that you'll get to a solution infuses the entire process with the energy and drive that you need to navigate the thorniest problems.

Human-centered designers are persistently focused on what could be, not the countless obstacles that may get in the way. Constraints are inevitable, and often they push designers toward unexpected solutions. But it's our core animating belief—that every problem is solvable—that shows just how deeply optimistic human-centered designers are.

Iterate, Iterate, Iterate

By iterating, we validate our ideas along the way because we're hearing from the people we're actually designing for.

—Gaby Brink, Founder, Tomorrow Partners

As human-centered designers, we adopt an iterative approach to solving problems because it makes feedback from the people we're designing for a critical part of how a solution evolves. By continually iterating, refining, and improving our work, we put ourselves in a place where we'll have more ideas, try a variety of approaches, unlock our creativity, and arrive more quickly at successful solutions.

Iteration keeps us nimble, responsive, and trains our focus on getting the idea and, after a few passes, every detail just right. If you aimed for perfection each time you built a prototype or shared an idea, you'd spend ages refining something whose validity was still in doubt. But by building, testing, and iterating, you can advance your idea without investing hours and resources until you're sure that it's the one.

At base, we iterate because we know that we won't get it right the first time. Or even the second. Iteration allows us the opportunity to explore, to get it wrong, to follow our hunches, but ultimately arrive at a solution that will be adopted and embraced. We iterate because it allows us to keep learning. Instead of hiding out in our workshops, betting that an idea, product, or service will be a hit, we quickly get out in the world and let the people we're designing for be our guides.

METHODS

INSPIRATION

The Inspiration phase is about learning on the fly, opening yourself up to creative possibilities, and trusting that as long as you remain grounded in desires of the communities you're engaging, your ideas will evolve into the right solutions. You'll build your team, get smart on your challenge, and talk to a staggering variety of people.

THIS PHASE WILL HELP YOU ANSWER
How do I get started?
How do I conduct an interview?
How do I keep people at the center of my research?
What are other tools I can use to understand people?

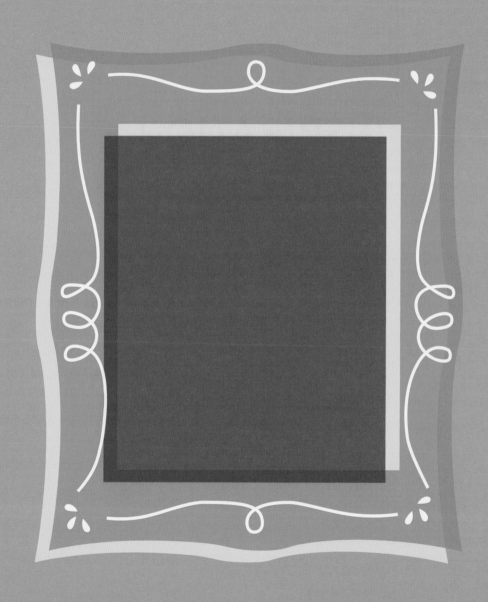

Frame Your Design Challenge

Properly framing your design challenge is critical to your success. Here's how to do it just right.

Getting the right frame on your design challenge will get you off on the right foot, organize how you think about your solution, and at moments of ambiguity, help clarify where you should push your design. Framing your design challenge is more art than science, but there are a few key things to keep in mind. First, ask yourself: Does my challenge drive toward ultimate impact, allow for a variety of solutions, and take into account context? Dial those in, and then refine it until it's the challenge you're excited to tackle.

STEPS

TIME
90 minutes

DIFFICULTY
Hard

WHAT YOU'LL NEED
Pen, Frame Your Design Challenge
worksheet p. 165

PARTICIPANTS
Design team

01 | Start by taking a first stab at writing your design challenge. It should be short and easy to remember, a single sentence that conveys what you want to do. We often phrase these as questions which set you and your team up to be solution-oriented and to generate lots of ideas along the way.

02 | Properly framed design challenges drive toward ultimate impact, allow for a variety of solutions, and take into account constraints and context. Now try articulating it again with those factors in mind.

03 | Another common pitfall when scoping a design challenge is going either too narrow or too broad. A narrowly scoped challenge won't offer enough room to explore creative solutions. And a broadly scoped challenge won't give you any idea where to start.

04 | Now that you've run your challenge through these filters, do it again. It may seem repetitive, but the right question is key to arriving at a good solution. A quick test we often run on a design challenge is to see if we can come up with five possible solutions in just a few minutes. If so, you're likely on the right track.

METHOD IN ACTION

Frame Your Design Challenge

It's rare that you'll Frame Your Design Challenge just right on the first try; at IDEO.org we often go through a number of revisions and lots of debate as we figure out precisely how to hone the problem we're looking to solve.

For the second challenge in our Amplify program, we knew that we wanted to focus on children's education, but needed to narrow the scope so that it would drive real impact, allow for a variety of solutions, and still give us enough context to get started. Challenge manager Chioma Ume described how she and her team sharpened the challenge.

"We knew we wanted to do something around kids, but of course we then have to ascertain which kids. Should it be all kids, just teens, young kids? Because of the tremendous importance of early childhood development, we settled on children, ages zero to five. But we certainly didn't start knowing that we'd focus just on them."

Even then, the challenge needed refinement. By eventually landing not on children, but their parents, the team and its partners at the UK's Department for International Development, crafted a brief that it thought would have the most impact.

"We chose to focus on the people closest to children, their parents," says Ume. But she stresses that though parents became the focus, the children remained the beneficiaries, a nuance that would keep the team from spinning off or focusing too

heavily on improving parents' lives. In the end, the team arrived at a well framed challenge, one that asks: How might parents in low-income communities ensure children thrive in their first five years?

Use the Frame Your Design Challenge worksheet on p. 165 and take multiple passes to make sure that your question drives at impact, gives you a starting place, but still is broad enough to allow for a great variety of creative answers.

Frame Your Design Challenge

What is the problem you're trying to solve?

Improving the lives of children.

1) Take a stab at framing it as a design question.

How might we improve the lives of children?

2) Now, state the ultimate impact you're trying to have.

We want very young children in low-income communities to thrive.

3) What are some possible solutions to your problem?
Think broadly. It's fine to start a project with a hunch or two, but make sure you allow for surprising outcomes.

Better nutrition, parents engaging with young kids to spur brain development, better education around

parenting, early childhood education centers, better access to neonatal care and vaccines.

4) Finally, write down some of the context and constraints that you're facing.
They could be geographic, technological, time-based, or have to do with the population you're trying to reach.

Because children aren't in control of their circumstances, we wanted to address our solution to their parents.

We want a solution that could work across different regions.

5) Does your original question need a tweak? Try it again.

How might parents in low-income communities ensure children thrive in their first five years.

Create a Project Plan

Get organized, understand your strengths, and start identifying what your team will need to come up with innovative solutions.

As you set out to solve your challenge, you'll need to create a plan. This gives you a chance to think through all the logistics of your project, and even though they're bound to change as things progress, you'll be in much better shape if you can plan for what's ahead. Reflect on your timeline, the space you'll work in, your staff, your budget, what skills you'll need, trips you'll take, and what you'll need to produce. Getting a good handle on all of this information can keep you on track.

STEPS

TIME
60-90 minutes

DIFFICULTY
Moderate

WHAT YOU'LL NEED
Pen, paper, Post-its, calendar

PARTICIPANTS
Design team

01 A good place to start is with a calendar. Print out or make a large one and put it up in your workspace. Now mark key dates. They could be deadlines, important meetings, travel dates, or times when your team members are unavailable.

02 Now that you've got a sense of your timeline, look at your budget and staff. Do you have everything that you'll need? If you foresee constraints, how can you get around them?

03 You'll need to get smart on your topic before you head into the field. Who should you talk to now? What will you need to read to be up to speed on your challenge?

04 Answer questions like: When should my team head into the field? Will my team make one visit or two? Will our partners be visiting? Will we need to physically make something? How much time, money, and manpower will we need to produce it?

05 Your project plan will change as things evolve, and that's perfectly OK. You can always amend things as you go but make sure that you're really thinking through your project before you start.

Build a Team

An <u>interdisciplinary mix of thinkers,</u> makers, and doers is just the right combination to tackle any design challenge.

Human-centered design works best with cross-disciplinary teams. You could put three business designers to work on a new social enterprise, but if you throw a graphic designer, a journalist, or an industrial designer into the mix, you're going to bring new modes of thinking to your team. It's smart to have a hunch about what kind of talent your team will need—if you're designing a social enterprise, a business designer is probably a good bet—but you won't get unexpected solutions with an expected team.

STEPS

TIME
60 minutes

DIFFICULTY
Hard

WHAT YOU'LL NEED
Pen, paper

PARTICIPANTS
Project lead, partner organizations

01 First, assess how many team members you'll need, your staff's availability, and when your project should start and end.

02 Look at the core members of your team and determine what they're good at and what they're not so good at.

03 Is there a clear <u>technical capability that you'll need</u> but don't <u>currently have</u>—maybe a mechanical engineer, a graphic designer, a skilled writer? Remember that <u>you can always add a team member for a shorter period of time</u> when <u>their skills</u> are most important.

Recruiting Tools

Human-centered design isn't just about talking to a lot of people, it's about talking to the right people. Build a strategy now so that your Interviews really count.

Before you start talking to the people you're designing for, it's important to have a strategy around who you talk to, what you ask them, and what pieces of information you need to gather. By planning ahead, and tracking who you talk to once you've done it, you can be sure to have the right balance of experts and laymen, women and men, people of different ethnicities and classes, as well as a full range of behaviors, beliefs, and perspectives.

STEPS

TIME
30-60 minutes

DIFFICULTY
Moderate

WHAT YOU'LL NEED
Pen, paper

PARTICIPANTS
Design team

01 As you start to determine who you want to talk to, think about a variety of factors: age, gender, ethnicity, class, social position. Who do you really need to hear from?

02 Be sensitive to gender when making your Interview plan. Some communities may not be comfortable with men interviewing women. Or if you're working on a touchy topic, like open defecation, make sure that you understand social dynamics before you begin your Interviews (p. 39).

03 Group Interviews (p. 42) can be a highly useful tool and also help you identify who you might like to speak more with in an individual Interview.

04 Refer to Extremes and Mainstreams (p. 49) to make sure that you're talking to a broad spectrum of people.

Secondary Research

Getting up to speed on your challenge is crucial to success in the field.

Human-centered design is all about talking with people about their challenges, ambitions, and constraints. But as you move through the Inspiration phase, there will be moments where you'll need more context, history, or data than a man-on-the-street style Interview can afford. Social sector challenges can be really thorny, which is why Secondary Research, whether done online, by reading books, or by crunching numbers, can help you ask the right questions. At IDEO.org, we find that a firm foundation of knowledge is the best place from which to tackle a design challenge.

TIME
1-2 days

DIFFICULTY
Moderate

WHAT YOU'LL NEED
Internet connection,
pen, notebook,
research materials

PARTICIPANTS
Design team

STEPS

01 Once you know your design challenge, it's time to start learning about its broader context. You can bone up quickly by exploring the most recent news in the field. Use the Internet, newspapers, magazines, or journals to know what's new.

02 Try to find recent innovations in your particular area. They could be technological, behavioral, or cultural. Understanding the edge of what's possible will help you ask great questions.

03 Take a look at other solutions in your area. Which ones worked? Which ones didn't? Are there any that feel similar to what you might design? Any solutions that have inspired you to make one of your own?

04 Because Interviews (p. 39) can be highly subjective, use your Secondary Research to get the facts and figures you'll need to understand the context of your challenge.

Interview

There's no better way to understand the hopes, desires, and aspirations of those you're designing for than by talking with them directly.

Interviews really are the crux of the Inspiration phase. Human-centered design is about getting to the people you're designing for and hearing from them in their own words. Interviews can be a bit daunting, but by following these steps below you'll unlock all kinds of insights and understanding that you'll never get sitting behind your desk. Whenever possible, conduct your Interviews in the person's space. You can learn so much about a person's mindset, behavior, and lifestyle by talking with them where they live or work.

STEPS

TIME
60-90 minutes

DIFFICULTY
Moderate

WHAT YOU'LL NEED
Pens, paper, Interview Guide worksheet p. 166

PARTICIPANTS
Design team, person you're designing for

01 No more than three research team members should attend any single Interview so as to not overwhelm the participant or crowd the location. Each team member should have a clear role (i.e. interviewer, note-taker, photographer).

02 Come prepared with a set of questions you'd like to ask. Start by asking broad questions about the person's life, values, and habits, before asking more specific questions that relate directly to your challenge.

03 Make sure to write down exactly what the person says, not what you think they might mean. This process is premised on hearing exactly what people are saying. If you're relying on a translator, make sure he or she understands that you want direct quotes, not the gist of what the person says.

04 What you hear is only one data point. Be sure to observe the person's body language and surroundings and see what you can learn from the context in which you're talking. Take pictures, provided you get permission first.

METHOD IN ACTION

Interview

One of the pillars of human-centered design is talking directly to the communities that you're looking to serve. And there's no better way to understand a person's desires, fears, and opinions on a given subject than by interviewing them.

In 2012, IDEO.org worked with the World Bank's Consultative Group to Assist the Poor (CGAP) and the bank Bancomer to identify opportunities for new and more accessible savings products to serve low-income Mexicans. The team conducted a ton of Interviews over the course of the project, each time trying to understand how people save their money. Again and again the team heard, "I don't save money." But after asking a few more questions they came to learn that low-income Mexicans may not think of their informal methods as savings in the way that a bank might, but they are certainly socking money away. And understanding how they do it was critical to the team's ultimate design.

Thanks to their Interviews, the team learned that one man stashed extra money in the pockets of his shirts when he hung them in the closet. Another woman gave money to her grandmother because she knew that she wouldn't let her spend it on something frivolous. Still another woman parcelled her money out in coffee cans dedicated to various expenses like school fees, food, and rent.

The team even talked to one man who saved his money in bricks. He was "saving" to build a house so he put his extra money in building supplies and then, after a few years, constructed the house.

A key insight that came out of these interviews was that many low-income Mexicans don't save for saving's sake, they save for particular things. This idea led directly to the team designing a project-based approach to savings, aptly dubbed "Mis Proyectos" (My Projects).

Try to conduct your Interviews in the homes or offices of the people you're designing for. Put them at ease first by asking more general questions before getting specific. And be sure to ask open-ended questions instead of yes-or-no questions.

Interview Guide

Open General
What are some broad questions you can ask to open the conversation and warm people up?

What kind of job do you have?

How are you paid?

How do you save for the future?

Then Go Deep
What are some questions that can help you start to understand this person's hopes, fears, and ambitions?

How do you allocate your money now?

Where do you actually keep the money you want to put aside?

What helps you save money?

If you've visited a bank, tell us about your experience.

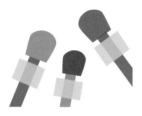

Group Interview

You can come to a quick understanding of a community's life, dynamics, and needs by conducting a Group Interview.

Though a Group Interview may not offer the depth of an individual Interview (p. 39) in someone's home, it can give you a compelling look at how a larger set of the people you're designing for operates. The best Group Interviews seek to hear everyone's voice, get diverse opinions, and are strategic about group makeup. For example, an all-female group might give you insight into the role of women in a society whereas a mixed group may not. If you're looking to learn quickly what is valuable to a community, Group Interviews are a great place to start.

STEPS

TIME
90-120 minutes

DIFFICULTY
Moderate

WHAT YOU'LL NEED
Pens, paper, camera

PARTICIPANTS
At least 2 members of the design team, 7-10 people you're designing for

01 | Identify the sort of group you want to talk with. If you're trying to learn something specific, organize the group so that they're likely to have good answers to the questions that you've got.

02 | Convene the Group Interview on neutral ground, perhaps a shared community space that people of all ages, races, and genders can access.

03 | In a Group Interview, be certain to have one person asking the questions and other team members taking notes and capturing what the group is saying.

04 | Come prepared with a strategy to engage the quieter members of the group. This can mean asking them questions directly or finding ways to make the more vocal members of the group recede for a moment.

05 | Group Interviews are a great setting to identify who you might want to go deeper with in a Co-Creation Session (p. 109).

Expert Interview

Experts can fill you in quickly on a topic, and give you key insights into relevant history, context, and innovations.

Though the crux of the Inspiration phase is talking with the people you're designing for, you can gain valuable perspective by talking to experts. Experts can often give you a systems-level view of your project area, tell you about recent innovations—successes and failures—and offer the perspectives of organizations like banks, governments, or NGOs. You might also look to experts for specific technical advice.

STEPS

TIME
60-90 minutes

DIFFICULTY
Moderate

WHAT YOU'LL NEED
Pens, camera, notebook

PARTICIPANTS
Design team, expert

01 | Determine what kind of expert you need. If you're working in agriculture, perhaps an agronomist. In reproductive health? A doctor or policymaker may be a good bet.

02 | When recruiting your experts, give them a preview of the kinds of questions you'll be asking and let them know how much of their time you'll need.

03 | Choose experts with varying points of view. You don't want the same opinions over and over.

04 | Ask smart, researched questions. Though you should come prepared with an idea of what you'd like to learn, make sure your game plan is flexible enough to allow you to pursue unexpected lines of inquiry.

05 | Record your Expert Interview with whatever tools you have. A pen and paper work fine.

Define Your Audience

Consider the broad spectrum of people who will be touched by your design solution.

Before you dig into your in-context research, it's critical to know who you're designing for. You're bound to learn more once you're in the field, but having an idea of your target audience's needs, contexts, and history will help ensure that you start your research by asking smart questions. And don't limit your thinking just to the people you're designing for. You may need to consider governments, NGOs, other businesses, or competitors.

STEPS

TIME
30-60 minutes

DIFFICULTY
Easy

WHAT YOU'LL NEED
Pen, paper, Post-its

PARTICIPANTS
Design team

01 With your team, write down the people or groups that are directly involved in or reached by your project. Are you designing for children? For farmers? Write all the groups down on Post-its and put them on a wall so you can visualize your audience.

02 Now add people or groups who are peripherally relevant, or are associated with your direct audience.

03 Think about the connections these people have with your topic. Who are the fans? Who are the skeptics? Who do you most need on your side? Add them to the wall.

04 Now arrange these Post-its into a map of the people involved in your challenge. Save it and refer to it as you move through the Inspiration phase.

Conversation Starters

Conversation Starters put a bunch of ideas in front of a person and seek to spark their reactions.

Conversation Starters are a great way to get a reaction and begin a dialogue. The idea here is to suggest a bunch of ideas around a central theme to the people you're designing for and then see how they react. The ideas you generate for your Conversation Starters are totally sacrificial, so if they don't work, drop them and move on. The goal here is to encourage creativity and outside-the-box thinking from the people you're designing for.

STEPS

TIME
30-60 minutes

DIFFICULTY
Moderate

WHAT YOU'LL NEED
Pens, notebook

PARTICIPANTS
Design team, people you're designing for

01 Determine what you want the people you're designing for to react to. If you're designing a sanitation system you might come up with a bunch of Conversation Starters around toilets or privacy.

02 Now come up with many ideas that could get the conversation started. What is the toilet of the future, the toilet of the past, a super toilet, the president's toilet? Come up with a list of ideas like this to share with the person you're designing for.

03 Once you're with the person you're designing for, start by telling them that you're interested in their reactions to these Conversation Starters. Some may be silly, some may be absurd, you're only looking to get their opinions.

04 As the person you're designing for shares her take on your Conversation Starters, be open to however she interprets the concepts. When one of them strikes her, ask more questions. You can learn a lot about how she thinks and what she might want out of your solution.

METHOD IN ACTION

Conversation Starters

The name says it all: Conversation Starters are meant to do just that. But beyond getting the person you're designing for talking, the goal is to get them thinking. This Method is a great way to open a person up to creative thinking and to then learn more about her attitudes about the subject.

An IDEO.org design team working in Uganda with Ugafode and the Mennonite Economic Development Associates on how to design formal savings tools for low-income Ugandans used Conversation Starters to plumb how Ugandans felt about banks. By presenting them with very basic ideas about banks and then soliciting a response, the team came to some pretty compelling insights.

They learned that some Ugandans thought banks were only for "big money," and not the small sums that they might otherwise be dealing in. Another person told the team that he wants his money working for the community, a benefit that he did not think would happen if it were sitting in a bank.

The big insight that came from the dialogue that the Conversation Starters sparked was that Ugandans are currently using all manner of informal savings devices. And for a bank to work in this community, it would have to play alongside, not necessarily replace, the existing informal services and systems on which people rely.

When you're using Conversation Starters, remember that the goal is to get people talking. If the person you're talking to doesn't have much of a response to one, move right onto the next. Keep going until you find something that works, then keep the conversation going with open-ended questions. Premade cards are a great device to get the conversation started and give people something to react to. This is also a chance to get people thinking creatively so feel free to ask outlandish questions to keep the conversation flowing.

These Conversation Starter cards helped an IDEO.org team working in Uganda better understand local financial habits.

The Loan Surprise Game

There are all kinds of ways that you can learn from the communities you're looking to serve. An IDEO.org team working on designing mobile financial tools to help victims of Typhoon Yolanda in the Philippines devised an ingenious way to understand how people felt about getting loans. They made a board game.

In the Loan Surprise Game, the team set up shop in an area where they knew lots of the people they were designing for would congregate and then laid out a simple dice game where you would "roll" a loan. Once a participant rolled the dice, she was told the terms of the loan and asked if she'd take it.

On the first day they ran it, the goal of the game wasn't to actually design financial products on the spot, but to grasp how members of this community felt about loans and what factors made them willing to take them on. The team learned about how bank loans were perceived as inaccessible to those with little income, but also how getting money from a loan shark was easy, but caused significant anxiety. They also used the game to probe deeper into what kind of financial support people most wanted. By getting participants to change some of the variables, they were able to see what kind of loans were attractive and which sort would never work.

On the second day of the Loan Surprise Game the team actually moved from research to prototyping by adding loan options and qualifications. It was a way to ask more profound questions about how people would actually borrow money, and most importantly, it got people talking. By putting scenarios in front of people and getting their reactions, you quickly engage them in your research and create an opportunity to deeply understand what they want, fear, and need.

Extremes and Mainstreams

Designing a solution that will work for everyone means talking to both extreme users and those squarely in the middle of your target audience.

When recruiting people to Interview (p. 39), go after both the big broad mainstream and those on either extreme of the spectrum. An idea that suits an extreme user will nearly certainly work for the majority of others. And without understanding what people on the far reaches of your solution need, you'll never arrive at answers that can work for everyone. More importantly, talking to people at the extreme end of your product or service can spark your creativity by exposing you to use cases, hacks, and design opportunities that you'd never have imagined.

STEPS

TIME
30-60 minutes

DIFFICULTY
Moderate

WHAT YOU'LL NEED
Pens, notebook

PARTICIPANTS
Design team, people you're designing for

01 | Think about all the different people who might use your solution. Extremes can fall on a number of spectrums and you'll want variety. Maybe you'll want to talk to someone who lives alone and someone who lives with a large extended family. Maybe you'll want to talk to both the elderly and children. Each will offer a take on your project that can spur new thinking.

02 | When you talk to an extreme, ask them how they would use your solution. Ask them if they use something similar now and how it does or does not suit their needs.

03 | Select appropriate community contacts to help arrange meetings and individual Interviews. Make sure you're talking to men and women. You might even stumble across an extreme user in another context and want to talk to them there.

04 | Be sensitive to certain extremes when you Interview them. They may often be left out of discussions like these so make them feel welcome and let them know that their voices are critical to your research.

Extremes and Mainstreams

Though extreme users can spur all kinds of new thinking, each specific project will dictate who you should talk to. There are certain factors you should always take into account, like gender, age, income level, and social status. But make sure that your particular challenge leads you to more nuanced extremes. If you're working on delivering clean water, you'll want to talk with people who have to travel especially long distances to get it, or perhaps people who used to seek clean water but have stopped. What constitutes an extreme user will vary, but your commitment to talking with them shouldn't.

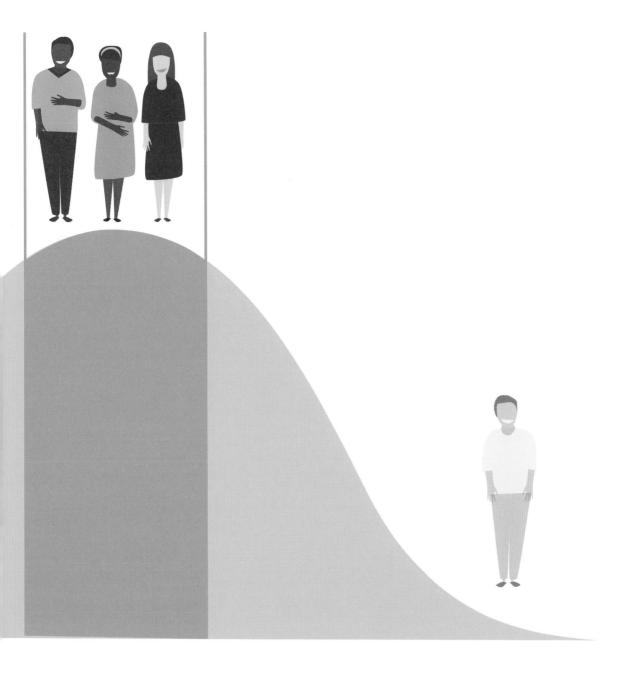

Immersion

There's no better way to understand the people you're designing for than by immersing yourself in their lives and communities.

The Inspiration phase is dedicated to hearing the voices and understanding the lives of the people you're designing for. The best route to gaining that understanding is to talk to them in person, where they live, work, and lead their lives. Once you're in-context, there are lots of ways to observe the people you're designing for. Spend a day shadowing them, have them walk you through how they make decisions, play fly on the wall and observe them as they cook, socialize, visit the doctor—whatever is relevant to your challenge.

STEPS

TIME
Ideally a full week

DIFFICULTY
Hard

WHAT YOU'LL NEED
If you're going into the field you'll need travel and accommodation

PARTICIPANTS
Design team, people you're designing for

01 | As you Create a Project Plan (p. 34), budget enough time and money to send team members into the field to spend time with the people you're designing for. Try to organize a homestay if possible.

02 | Once you're there, observe as much as you can. It's crucial to record exactly what you see and hear. It's easy to interpret what's in front of you before you've fully understood it, so be sure you're taking down concrete details and quotes alongside your impressions.

03 | A great Immersion technique is to shadow a person you're designing for a day. Ask them all about their lives, how they make decisions, watch them socialize, work, and relax.

04 | If you've got a shorter window for Immersion, you can still learn a lot by following someone for a few hours. Pay close attention to the person's surroundings. You can learn a lot from them.

Analogous Inspiration

To get a fresh perspective on your research, shift your focus to a new context.

IDEO.org teams are often led by their intuition to take creative leaps. It may feel silly to visit an Apple store when you're designing for those living in difficult circumstances, but you may unlock the key to a memorable customer experience or a compelling way to arrange products. Analogous settings can help you isolate elements of an experience, interaction, or product, and then apply them to whatever design challenge you're working on. Besides, getting out from behind your desk and into a new situation is always a great way to spur creative thinking.

STEPS

TIME
30-60 minutes

DIFFICULTY
Moderate

WHAT YOU'LL NEED
Pens, paper, camera

PARTICIPANTS
Design team, contact in the analogous setting

01 | On a large sheet of paper, list the distinct activities, behaviors, and emotions you're looking to research.

02 | Next to each one, write down a setting or situation where you might observe this activity, behavior, or emotion. For example, if the activity is "use a device at the same time every day," parallel situations might be how people use alarm clocks.

03 | Have the team vote on the site visits that they would like to observe for inspiration and arrange for an observation visit.

04 | When you make your visit, pay close attention to what it is you want to understand, but remain open to all kinds of other inspiration.

METHOD IN ACTION

Analogous Inspiration

As part of a three-month engagement to increase mobile money use in Ghana, IDEO.org partnered with Tigo, a telecommunications company, and the World Bank's Consultative Group to Assist the Poor (CGAP). The design team's goal was to help our partners improve their existing mobile tools enabling both increased customer activity and service adoption. Improving the reach of these tools among low-income communities would provide better access to formal money management opportunities and reach those who are typically unbanked.

During the Inspiration phase, the team started to hear a few ideas again and again. They realized that for unbanked Ghanaians, there was quite a bit of value for consumers in seeing a visible community of users of whatever product or service they designed.

As the team delved deeper into what visible community meant, it sought analogous examples. By examining other visible communities, like Arsenal Football Club fans in England, Lyft drivers in the United States, and Catholics celebrating Ash Wednesday, the team fleshed out an insight that ultimately drove the design.

By the end of the project, the notion that visible community could drive adoption was a key piece of the research, and it wouldn't have had the same depth if the design team hadn't dug into other visible communities to understand what makes them tick. As the team's research around visible community got deeper, they came to see that evidence of participation, public displays of identity, and support from the community were keys to a successful solution.

When you're identifying analogous examples, try to drill down to your core insights. What characteristics are you exploring? Instead of trying to come up with one analogy to match everything that your design challenge encompasses, try thinking about it in terms of its components.

Arsenal Football Club fans (top), Catholics on Ash Wednesday (bottom right), and the American car service Lyft (bottom left) all provided Analogous Inspiration for a team working to understand visible communities.

Card Sort

This simple exercise will help you identify what's most important to the people you're designing for.

A Card Sort is a quick and easy way to spark conversation about what matters most to people. By putting a deck of cards, each with a word or single image, in someone's hands and then asking them to rank them in order of preference, you'll gain huge insight into what really counts. You can also use the Card Sort exercise to start a deeper conversation about what a person values and why.

STEPS

TIME
30 minutes

DIFFICULTY
Easy

WHAT YOU'LL NEED
Premade cards on p. 168 or your own cards

PARTICIPANTS
Design team, person you're designing for

01 Make your own deck of cards or use the cards provided in the Resources section on p. 168. If you're making your own cards, use either a word or a picture on each card. Whatever you select, make sure that it's easy to understand. Pictures are a better choice if the person doing the Card Sort speaks another language or cannot read.

02 When tailoring your deck of cards to your precise research objectives, be sure that you're mixing concrete ideas with more abstract ones. You can learn a lot about how the person you're designing for understands the world by making this exercise more than just a simple ranking.

03 Now give the cards to the person you're designing for and ask her to sort them according to what's most important.

04 There are a couple variations on this Method that work nicely: Instead of asking the person you're designing for to rank the cards in order of preference, ask her to arrange them as she sees fit. The results might surprise you. Another tweak is to pose different scenarios. Ask the person you're designing for how she would sort the cards if she had more money, if she were old, if she lived in a big city.

METHOD IN ACTION

Card Sort

While working in India on a solar energy project with d.light, an IDEO.org design team set out to design the next generation of solar-powered lights for rural, low-income communities. To prompt people to think about their needs and experiences in a new way, the design team used an activity called Card Sort. Card Sorts can be done in a number of different ways, and in this case the team presented the community with a deck of cards showing all different types of animals.

It may sound crazy at the outset, but the team came to a key insight shortly after it laid out the animal cards in front of a community member and then asked, "what animal does this solar light represent to you?"

Time and again, the team found that people compared the solar lamp to a chicken or a cow. The team quickly realized that chickens and cows are considered great assets. Chickens keep producing eggs and cows keep producing milk long after you purchase them. Had community members compared the light to an eagle or snake, the team would have questioned whether it was the right product for the market. But by coming to see that people understood the value proposition of a solar-powered light, they knew they were on the right

track. The chicken analogy also gave the team language to use to help talk about the benefit of the light in a subsequent communications strategy.

You can do a Card Sort with all kinds of cards, and you needn't go as abstract as the animal cards if they don't suit your needs. Try the sample cards in the Resources section on p. 168 to get started. And feel free to tailor the deck to your own needs.

By running a Card Sort, an IDEO.org team uncovered how this community in India thinks about solar lights.

Peers Observing Peers

Get a glimpse into the community you're designing for by seeing how they document their own lives.

You'll be talking to a lot of people as part of the Inspiration phase, but learning from the people you're designing for can also mean empowering them to do some of the research themselves and then share back with you. You may also find that social and gender dynamics, or research around a sensitive subject, like sexual health for example, may limit how much the people you're designing for are willing to tell you. By bringing the people you're designing for in as partners in your research and giving them the tools to capture their own attitudes and hopes, you'll learn more than you ever could on your own.

STEPS

TIME
2-4 hours

DIFFICULTY
Moderate

WHAT YOU'LL NEED
Pens, paper, camera,
art supplies

PARTICIPANTS
Design team, person you're
designing for

01 | There are a number of ways you can get a person you're designing for to observe and document her peers and community. Start by determining how you want to learn. It could be through Interviews (p. 39), photos, Collages (p. 61), Card Sorts (p. 57), etc.

02 | Outfit the person you're designing for with what she'll need—a camera perhaps, art supplies, a notebook pen—and take her through the observation and reporting process.

03 | Offer support throughout the observation and reporting process. Make certain that she knows that there is no right answer and that you only want the honest opinions, hopes, and fears of the people she talks to.

04 | When she's done, collect what she's produced, but also be sure to Interview her about how the process went. You'll want more than just the facts, so be sure to find out what surprised or inspired her, how her opinions might have changed, and what she learned about her peers.

Collage

Having the people you're designing for make and explain a collage can help you understand their values and thought process.

Making things is a fantastic way to think things through, one that we use at IDEO.org to unlock creativity and push ourselves to new and innovative places. Getting the people you're designing for to make things can help you understand how they think, what they value, and may surface unexpected themes and needs. Collages are an easy, low-fidelity way to push people to make something tangible and then to explain what it means to them.

STEPS

TIME
30-60 minutes

DIFFICULTY
Easy

WHAT YOU'LL NEED
Pens, paper, glue, magazines

PARTICIPANTS
Design team, people you're designing for

01 When you meet the people you're designing for, make sure you have Collage supplies with you.

02 Give the people you're designing for a prompt for their Collage. Perhaps you ask them to make a Collage that represents taking control of their lives, their dream jobs, or how they think about their families.

03 When they're finished, ask them to describe the Collage, what the various elements represent, and how it speaks to the prompt. Not only will you have a visual record of your research, but you can use the Collage as a springboard to further conversation or to explore new areas in your research.

METHOD IN ACTION

Collage

A team at IDEO.org was asked to help create a marketing strategy for a partner that sells health insurance through a mobile money platform in rural Nigeria. The team wanted to co-design the messaging with its audience, but worried that explaining the service could get confusing. Most of the audience had never heard of health insurance, much less mobile money. So the team decided to start with the most basic explanation and let the community help devise a campaign from there. And they did it through an incredibly simple research tool: a Collage.

They asked 25 workshop participants to show them what "community health" looks like. The team picked the term "community health" because it felt like the ultimate goal of the service that they wanted to market. Then they provided images, words, and magazines and told the participants simply to create something.

Going into this process, the team assumed that its audience would want to see medical imagery like doctors, clinics, and medications—images that spoke to the credibly of the service. What surprised them, however, was that community health was far more nuanced in the minds of this group. People were drawn to images of marketplaces, fruits and vegetables, exercise, families, and community events. When the team asked people to explain why they chose these images, they said that health

goes far beyond having access to modern medicine. They told the team that any product promoting better healthcare should consider what makes a healthy lifestyle, not just a trip to the doctor's office.

This mentality of holistic health applied to the messaging the team provided as well. In particular people were drawn to the phrase, "invest in your health and strengthen your community." This was because "health insurance" had an entirely different connotation than it often does in the United States, instead of being perceived as coverage for worst-case scenarios, many people thought of it as a community health pool that an individual bought into, which everyone would eventually benefit from over time. This very conception of health insurance ended up at the center of the final marketing strategy. It's something the team likely wouldn't have discovered without this Collage exercise.

Here are a few good tricks to keep in mind when you're having people Collage: Make sure that your prompt is simple, yet evocative. It's also best if the magazines they're working with are full of pictures, have some relevance to the topic you looking to learn more about, and are purchased locally. You can also print some key words or phrases if you want to test a particular message.

The Collages this group made helped an IDEO.org team understand what "community health" means in rural Nigeria.

Guided Tour

Taking a Guided Tour through the home or workplace of the person you're designing for can reveal their habits and values.

A Guided Tour is a great method to employ when you're in the field. Immersion (p. 52) is one of the primary ways we learn about the people we're designing for at IDEO.org. Having one of them give you a Guided Tour of their home, workplace, or daily activities will reveal not just the physical details of the person's life, but the routines and habits that animate it.

STEPS

TIME
2-4 hours

DIFFICULTY
Moderate

WHAT YOU'LL NEED
Pens, paper, camera

PARTICIPANTS
Design team, person you're designing for

01 | Arrange with someone you're designing for to get a Guided Tour of her home or workplace. Cultural and gender dynamics may come into play when you visit someone's home, so be sensitive to those issues and make sure you've got full permission before your visit.

02 | Come with just two team members, one to ask questions and the other to take notes. Pay close attention to the space that you're visiting, the rituals you see there, what's on the walls, who uses it, and where it's located. All are key pieces of information.

03 | Only take photos if you can get permission.

04 | Ask lots of questions about the person's habits and space. Why does she do the things she does? Who uses the space? Where are things kept? Why are things organized the way that they are?

Draw It

Spur deeper and different kinds of conversations by picking up a pen and paper and drawing.

Drawing is a great way to learn from the people you're designing for. Whether it's you with the pen or them, a quick sketch, a graph, or a timeline is a fantastic way to bridge language barriers and keep a record of your research. Drawing can also help the person you're designing for organize her thoughts visually and spark ideas and conversation in a different way than talking. For example, you may ask someone to draw everything they spend money on in a week, or map out all the jobs they've had, or show you the route they take to their job.

STEPS

TIME
30 minutes

DIFFICULTY
Easy

WHAT YOU'LL NEED
Pens, notebook

PARTICIPANTS
Design team, person you're designing for

01 | Make sure you have a pen and paper handy when talking with the people you're designing for. Even a sheet torn out of your notebook works great.

02 | When you want the person you're designing for to draw something, give them a clear idea of what you're after. A map of their daily route? A timeline of their annual income? What percentage of their fields are dedicated to a certain crop?

03 | The person you're designing for may feel intimidated or that she's not a good artist. Help her over that fear. Or be the one to draw first so that she doesn't feel embarrassed.

04 | You can use the drawings as Conversation Starters (p. 45). This Method can get you to a deeper understanding of the person you're designing for so investigate what they've drawn.

In-Context Research

At IDEO.org, we've found that the best way to really build empathy with the people you're designing for is to immerse yourself in their worlds. So when one of our teams set out to design a mobile app to help the Chicago nonprofit Moneythink reinforce good financial habits among low-income teens, our designers immediately packed their bags and headed for Illinois.

The design team started by attending the classes that Moneythink offers in a handful of Chicago schools, talking with students, and interviewing them about their personal finances, what kind of tools they use, and how money flows in and out of their lives.

But in-context immersion means far more than attending class with the people you're designing for. It means fully understanding and experiencing the circumstances of their lives.

So the team toured the neighborhoods where many of the Moneythink students live. It visited check-cashing stores and prepaid mobile phone stores to start to understand the kinds of financial services on offer to this low-income community. And perhaps most important when determining what kind of app to design, the team immersed itself in the social apps Moneythink students use most.

"I wasn't even on Instagram until this project," says designer Rafael Smith, a perfect example of how human-centered designers meet communities where they are. The team quickly moved on to Kik, Snapchat, and others to fully grasp how these teens use their phones and to help inform how they might prototype their designs.

By immersing themselves in the Moneythink students' lives—both physical and digital—the team came to key insights. They noticed that money for these teens was highly social—it came in on birthdays, for example, and flowed out while in the company of friends. The team realized that by adding a social component to the app (a la Snapchat or Instagram) they could make what is meant to be a teaching tool feel far more relevant and help drive toward better financial habits.

Resource Flow

By organizing and visualizing how a person or family spends money, you'll see how it comes in, goes out, and opportunities for more efficiency in the system.

A Resource Flow is an exercise you can try while you're conducting an Interview (p. 39). It consists of listing—or better, drawing—every asset that comes into a household and how those assets are spent. Remember that assets aren't always money, so be sure to include livestock, seeds, labor, and the like. Likewise, not every payment is perceived as such. Obligatory giving, charity, and care for family members might not seem like a payment, but should be considered.

STEPS

TIME
30 minutes

DIFFICULTY
Easy

WHAT YOU'LL NEED
Pens, Resource Flow worksheet p. 167

PARTICIPANTS
Design team, person you're designing for

01 | See if any of the people you're Interviewing want to draw. If so, let them. If not you can do it as well.

02 | List or draw everything that brings money into the house. Remember that assets may not always be currency.

03 | Now list or draw everything that takes money out of the household.

04 | Start asking questions about what you see. What's the most expensive thing he buys, what can't he live without, what is there never enough money for? Have the person you're designing for rank both inputs and outputs in terms of value. Find out how frequently money comes in and goes out. Use the lists to get a full picture of their finances.

05 | A nice additional step is to map these inputs and outputs on a calendar. You might find that money comes in all at once but has to be paid out bit by bit. Or that though you're not talking to a farmer, her income may be tied to an agricultural cycle.

METHOD IN ACTION

Resource Flow

When working with Arohana in Southern India to explore microfranchise opportunities, it was crucial for an IDEO.org design team to better understand the financial lives of local farmers and their communities.

Arohana is a social enterprise that supports small-scale dairy producers by collecting their milk and creating a stable market. When partnering with IDEO.org, the design team was asked to help Arohana think about how they might expand services to clients beyond just dairy farming through an equipment leasing model. One major goal of the project was to support rural women in the adoption of more modern, mechanized agricultural practices.

On a visit to Thanjavur, India, the IDEO.org team sought to learn as much as possible about the financial awareness and decision making of local farmers and their families through an exercise called Resource Flow. In this exercise, they learned what revenues a typical farmer would see and then what their costs looked like—from both seasonal farming inputs, such as seeds or animal feed, to monthly household costs, like school fees. Sometimes the full picture went well beyond just the farm, with family members bringing money into the household from unexpected or informal jobs as well. By taking the numbers out of the equation and talking in terms of the real items

and services that people deal with on a day-to-day basis, the team gained an accurate picture of farmers' financial lives.

After using this activity and talking with a number of farmers, the design team came to a number of insights about the current state of rural agriculture and micro business. For example, though many initial conversations with farmers pointed to tractors as the primary request when it came to farming equipment, it was found that they were far less economically feasible than smaller tools like sprayers. The costs and profits of leasing smaller tools fit into a farmer's Resource Flow without straining it to the point of financial instability.

Use the Resource Flow worksheet on p. 167 to fill out your own.

Resource Flow

For Interviews:

What brings money in?

1 cow
2 pigs
Sewing business
10 chickens
1 hectare maize
0.5 hectare potato

Where does money go?

School fees
Transportation
Medical bills
Seed
Fertilizer
Labor
Animal feed
Sewing materials

Case Study: Vroom

A Human-Centered Take on Early Childhood Development

Advances in neuroscience and child development confirm what many educators have long believed: Children's readiness for kindergarten (and life beyond) hinges on positive engagement with their parents and caregivers during the first five years of their lives. This is the most active period for brain development, when children's brains form new connections at a rate of 700 synapses per second. But as a society, America underinvests in children and families during the earliest years, leaving far too much opportunity on the table. For low-income parents, who may have lacked good models themselves and may feel judged or blamed, much parenting advice is unattainable.

The Bezos Family Foundation and IDEO.org set out to activate engagement through new tools and messages, and to broaden the prescription beyond commonly heard (but not uniformly embraced) directives about reading to children. Could there be a way to communicate brain science directly to parents in ways that positively influence behavior, and raises the value of all forms of positive interaction with babies and toddlers?

DESIGN TEAM
2 IDEO.org designers

PARTNERS
Bezos Family Foundation

TIMELINE
Design phase 14 weeks; to Vroom
launch 3 years

LOCATION
Across the USA

THE OUTCOME

After extensive interviews with parents, child development experts, and pediatricians around the country, the IDEO.org team developed a large-scale messaging campaign celebrating everyday moments as learning opportunities. Whether sitting in the laundromat or shopping at the supermarket, the fundamental message was that taking advantage of the many chances to engage with a child strengthens the foundation of that child's brain development. The Bezos Family Foundation built upon our design team's key insights, further developed them, and in the spring of 2014, launched Vroom. Vroom advocates for the time parents do have and using it in different ways to help build their kids' brains.

INSPIRATION

The IDEO.org team undertook a highly immersive Inspiration phase, visiting low-income communities in California, New York, and Pennsylvania to conduct interviews with parents and to observe existing programs aimed at improving child development outcomes. The team learned that many of the parents they met had very tough upbringings. These parents didn't feel fully equipped to engage with their children, because their own parents may not have engaged with them. One of the most successful programs the team witnessed during their research was one in which nurses went into people's homes for several hours each week simply to play with the children in front of the parents. By modeling play, they were able to affect behavior change and shift the parent-child dynamic.

Interviews with child development experts and pediatricians tended to reinforce the direct findings: If parenting advice is limited to reading books, those who don't feel comfortable reading aloud may forego all forms of engagement. One pediatrician in New York argued outright that playing, talking to, and responding to children even trumps reading.

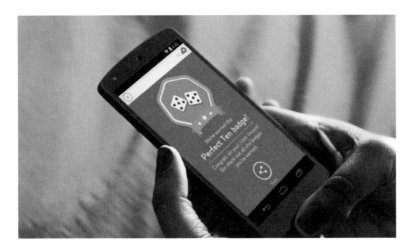

IDEATION

When field research was complete, the team returned to San Francisco to synthesize its findings and look for patterns among the interviews. As they synthesized everything they learned, the team began to formulate a voice, identity, and set of design principles for the campaign. They came to some core principles that still guide Vroom today, ideas like "speak in the voice of their peers," "withhold judgment," and "all parents want to be good parents."

The team came up with a series of personas, each of them representing a woman from the communities being served, then invited mothers to the office to review mood boards, listen to sample voices, and provide feedback on which character they'd trust for advice on child-rearing.

From this feedback period, the team discovered that most parents, though they weren't drawn to an academic approach to engaging their children, were very interested in the science behind behavior and brain development. Through a host of interviews, the team heard parents talking about a eureka moment after meeting with a neurologist who explained how the science worked. It was a revelation that had a big impact on how they saw their role in bringing up their children.

IMPLEMENTATION

By the end of the Inspiration and Ideation phases, the IDEO.org team had created a strong, well-defined creative brief that could be handed to an advertising agency and used as the foundation for a major campaign. They came up with provocations and prompts for people to play with their kids as well as an advertising strategy that included guerrilla interventions displayed in laundromats instead of on big billboards. After another couple years of refinement and more design work, the Bezos Family Foundation launched the pilot of Vroom in 2014 in King County, Washington.

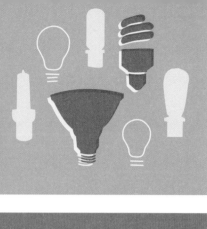
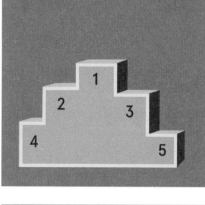

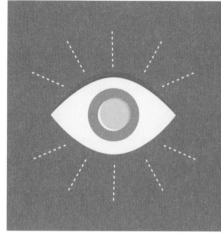

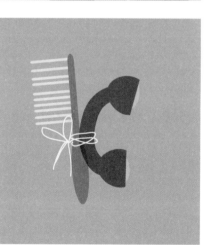
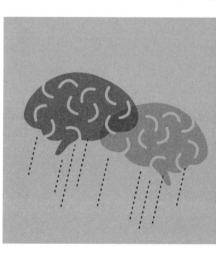
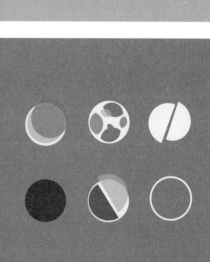
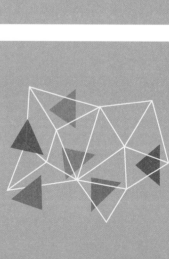

IDEATION

In the Ideation phase you'll share what you've learned with your team, make sense of a vast amount of data, and identify opportunities for design. You'll generate lots of ideas, some of which you'll keep, and others which you'll discard. You'll get tangible by building rough prototypes of your ideas, then you'll share them with the people from whom you've learned and get their feedback. You'll keep iterating, refining, and building until you're ready to get your solution out into the world.

THIS PHASE WILL HELP YOU ANSWER

How do I make sense of what I've learned?
How do I turn my learnings into an opportunity for design?
How do I make a prototype?
How do I know my idea is working?

Download Your Learnings

In the Inspiration phase you gathered tons of information. Here's how you share it with your team and put it to use.

Now that you've got a huge amount of notes, photos, impressions, and quotes, it's time to start making sense of them. Because teamwork is so critical to human-centered design, IDEO.org teams download their learnings as groups. One by one, you'll go around the room, capture your ideas and stories on Post-its, and put them on big sheets of paper. It's critical to pay close attention to your teammates' stories, learnings, and hunches. This is a rich and powerful way to share what you've heard and part of the goal is to make your individual learnings group knowledge.

STEPS

TIME
30 minutes per download

DIFFICULTY
Moderate

WHAT YOU'LL NEED
Pens, Post-its, a wall or board

PARTICIPANTS
Design team

01 | Take turns downloading. Start by getting rid of other distractions and sitting in a circle.

02 | When it's your turn, put all key information you want to share on Post-its and use them as you describe who you met, what you saw, the facts you gathered, and your impressions of the experience.

03 | Cluster the Post-its together as you put them on the wall or on a board so that you have a record of your discussion.

04 | When it's not your turn, pay close attention. Feel free to ask questions if something isn't clear.

05 | This process is best done the day of an Interview (p. 39) or after a day in the field. Download while your experiences and perceptions are fresh.

Share Inspiring Stories

Once you've had a chance to Download Your Learnings it's time to make sense of them. One way is to share the best of what you heard with your teammates.

Over the course of the Inspiration phase, you've heard stories or had experiences that stuck with you. Most likely, they won't be the ultimate solutions to your design challenge, but chances are they'll resonate with your team as well. At IDEO.org, we Share Inspiring Stories with our teammates so that they become part of our collective consciousness. The goal is to build a repository of stories for your team to draw from, tell, and retell. Capturing those powerful anecdotes and building them into the very narrative of your team's work helps everyone down the line.

STEPS

TIME
30-60 minutes

DIFFICULTY
Moderate

WHAT YOU'LL NEED
Pens, Post-its, a large sheet of paper, tape

PARTICIPANTS
Design team

01 | Affix a large piece of paper to the wall to capture all the team's Post-it notes and ideas from the story in one place.

02 | Tell the most compelling stories from the field to your teammates. Try to be both specific (talking about what actually happened) and descriptive (using physical senses to give texture to the description). Report on who, what, when, where, why, and how. And then invite each of your teammates to share their own inspiring stories.

03 | As you listen to your teammates' stories, write down notes and observations on Post-its. Use concise and complete sentences that everyone on your team can easily understand. Capture quotes, the person's life history, household details, income, aspirations, barriers, and any other observations.

04 | Write large enough so that everyone can read your notes. Then put all the Post-its up on the wall, organizing them into separate categories for each person that your team interviewed and each place that your team visited.

05 | At the end of story sharing, you'll have many sheets lined up on the wall with hundreds of Post-it notes. Consider this shared information as a group and start to own the most compelling stories you heard.

Top Five

This easy synthesis tool can help you prioritize, communicate, and strategize with your team.

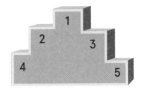

Ideation is a tough and heady phase of the human-centered design process. This exercise gives you a break from the deep thinking and simply asks, what are the Top Five ideas or themes sticking out to you right now. Not only can answering this question as a team help you strategize, but it can also help uncover themes, isolate key ideas, and reveal opportunities for design. Try using this method throughout the Ideation phase and you'll see how it can spark discussions or new thinking about anything from synthesis to prototyping to iteration.

STEPS

TIME
30 minutes

DIFFICULTY
Easy

WHAT YOU'LL NEED
Pens, Post-its

PARTICIPANTS
Design team

01 | Gather your team and have everyone write down the Top Five ideas jumping out at them.

02 | Share your Top Fives and cluster similar ideas. This is a great way to reveal what's most interesting or important at a given time.

03 | Consider doing this exercise often. And vary the time frame. What's your team's Top Five for the day? How about for the week? You can also use this tool to pull out the Top Five biggest challenges you face, or the Top Five crazy ideas you want to try.

04 | When it's not your turn, pay close attention. Feel free to ask questions if something isn't clear.

05 | Keeping and displaying the Post-its with your Top Fives is also a great way to watch your project evolve and to remind yourself of your priorities.

Find Themes

As you share your learnings with your team, patterns and themes are likely to emerge. Here's how to spot and make sense of them.

Once you've had a chance to Download Your Learnings (p. 77) and Share Inspiring Stories (p. 78), you're ready to Find Themes. Take a good long look across your Interviews (p. 39), Analogous Inspiration (p. 53), and other learnings. Have any patterns emerged? Is there a compelling insight you heard again and again? A consistent problem the people you're designing for face? What feels significant? What surprised you? These themes are bound to change, but as you move through the Ideation phase, continue to Find Themes and sort out what they mean.

STEPS

TIME
60-90 minutes

DIFFICULTY
Moderate

WHAT YOU'LL NEED
Your Post-its and boards from previous Ideation sessions

PARTICIPANTS
Design team

01 Gather your team around your Post-its from previous Ideation sessions. Move the most compelling, common, and inspiring quotes, stories, or ideas to a new board and sort them into categories.

02 Look for patterns and relationships between your categories and move the Post-its around as you continue grouping. The goal is to identify key themes and then to translate them into opportunities for design.

03 Arrange and rearrange the Post-its, discuss, debate, and talk through what's emerging. Don't stop until everyone is satisfied that the clusters represent rich opportunities for design.

04 Identifying these themes will help you Create Frameworks (p. 89) and write Design Principles (p. 105).

Create Insight Statements

A critical piece of the Ideation phase is plucking the insights that will drive your design out of the huge body of information you've gathered.

You've heard a lot from a lot of different people, downloaded learnings, and identified key themes from your research. The next step in the synthesis process is to Create Insight Statements, succinct sentences that will point the way forward. Insight statements are incredibly valuable as they'll help you frame How Might We (p. 85) questions and give shape and form to subsequent Brainstorms (p. 94). It's not always easy to create them, and it will probably take some work editing them down to the three to five main insights that will help you drive toward solutions.

STEPS

TIME
60 minutes

DIFFICULTY
Hard

WHAT YOU'LL NEED
Pens, Create Insight Statements worksheet p. 176, your work from Find Themes

PARTICIPANTS
Design team

01 | Take the themes that you identified in Find Themes (p. 80) and put them up on a wall or board.

02 | Now, take one of the themes and rephrase it as a short statement. You're not looking for a solution here, merely transforming a theme into what feels like a core insight of your research. This is a building block, not a resolved question.

03 | Once you've done this for all the themes, look back at your original design challenge. Sift through your insight statements and discard the ones that don't directly relate to your challenge. You only want three to five insights statements.

04 | Take another pass at refining your insights. Make sure that they convey the sense of a new perspective or possibility. Consider inviting someone who is not part of your team to read your insight statements and see how they resonate.

METHOD IN ACTION

Create Insight Statements

Working with Eram Scientific, an eToilet manufacturer in India, an IDEO.org team set out to help them make their electronic toilet experience more intuitive, user-friendly, and safe. Eram's eToilet is self-cleaning, coin-operated, and programmed to gather data on its usage, but there were key pieces of the user and brand experience that were ripe for a rethink.

The design team focused on Eram's target market in urban areas of southern India, and began their field research in Bangalore and Trivandrum. The team conducted over 100 interviews ranging from those who avoided using public toilets to frequent users. In addition, the team undertook extensive research with Eram staff, cleaning and service personnel, and even government officials.

Some key themes the team found were that cleanliness, reliability, and viability for women were the biggest concerns people had when making the choice to use a public toilet. The following worksheet shows some of the insights that this design team used as a starting point when identifying their opportunities for design. It's not an easy process, but one that your team will rely on as it drives toward an ultimate solution. You might take a couple stabs at forming your insight statements to get the hang of it.

Create Insight Statements

Write Your Design Challenge

Our design challenge is to make the eToilet experience more intuitive, user-friendly, and safe.

Theme: Women's needs

Insights:

1. Women want a private space in which to enter and exit the toilet.

2. Women greatly prefer single-sex toilets, but may still use unisex if they are clearly labeled.

3. Most women are forced to dispose of sanitary products by flushing them down the toilet.

Theme: Cleanliness

Insights:

1. Cleanliness is the defining quality of any toilet experience.

2. Without proper maintenance, toilets will become dirty very quickly.

3. Most people feel that free toilets are dirtier than paid ones, but many are still more likely to use a free toilet.

Theme: Reliability

Insights:

1. Reliability drives routine and gets people to return and use facilities frequently.

2. The people who live and work near a public toilet play a crucial role in directing users toward or away from it.

3. Most people care more about basic functionality than extra technology.

Explore Your Hunch

A huge part of human-centered design is following your nose. If you've got a feeling about something, give yourself a chance to explore it.

Human-centered design is an inherently intuitive process. And though a lot of the methodology is about arriving at new ideas you'd never dreamed of, you should always feel like you have the space to Explore Your Hunch. It could be an idea you had before the project started, or one that cropped up as you've been working. Either way, there are lots of ways to test your hunch, and you're destined to learn something when you do.

STEPS

TIME
30-60 minutes

DIFFICULTY
Moderate

WHAT YOU'LL NEED
Pens, Post-its, paper

PARTICIPANTS
Design team

01 | There are lots of ways to Explore Your Hunch. You could run a quick Brainstorm (p. 94). Or build a prototype. Or maybe run your idea past someone in an Expert Interview (p. 43).

02 | Start by articulating your hunch to your teammates and get their feedback. It could be that one of them is thinking along the same lines.

03 | Next, determine the best way to explore the idea. What do you need to uncover and understand to validate or disprove your idea?

04 | Remember that even if your hunch is wrong, there are still lots of learnings to be had. Remain open to them and capture them as you go.

How Might We

Translate your insight statements into opportunities for design by reframing them as "How Might We" questions.

By Finding Themes (p. 80) and Creating Insight Statements (p. 81), you've identified problem areas that pose challenges to the people you're designing for. Now, try reframing your insight statements as How Might We questions to turn those challenges into opportunities for design. We use the How Might We format because it suggests that a solution is possible and because they offer you the chance to answer them in a variety of ways. A properly framed How Might We doesn't suggest a particular solution, but gives you the perfect frame for innovative thinking.

STEPS

TIME
60 minutes

DIFFICULTY
Moderate

WHAT YOU'LL NEED
Insight statements, pens,
Create How Might We Questions
worksheet p. 177

PARTICIPANTS
Design team

01 | Start by looking at the insight statements that you've created. Try rephrasing them as questions by adding "How might we" at the beginning. Use the worksheet on p. 177.

02 | The goal is to find opportunities for design, so if your insights suggest several How Might We questions that's great.

03 | Now take a look at your How Might We question and ask yourself if it allows for a variety of solutions. If it doesn't, broaden it. Your How Might We should generate a number of possible answers and will become a launchpad for your Brainstorms (p. 94).

04 | Finally, make sure that your How Might We's aren't too broad. It's a tricky process but a good How Might We should give you both a narrow enough frame to let you know where to start your Brainstorm, but also enough breadth to give you room to explore wild ideas.

METHOD IN ACTION

How Might We

As you may recall from the example that accompanies Create Insight Statements (p. 81), IDEO.org partnered with Eram Scientific, an eToilet manufacturer in Southern India, to make their electronic toilet more intuitive, user-friendly, and safe.

Identifying key insights started the team down the path of finding opportunities for design. The next step was to reframe those insights as generative questions. Review the Create Insight Statements worksheet on p. 83 and then take a look at the How Might We questions (on the next page) that the team created from their insights.

Further thinking and eventually tangible design solutions emerged from many of these How Might We's. For instance, the team answered the first gender-focused question by coming up with a small L-shaped wall outside the door of the toilet. When prototyping this addition, the team heard from women who said that they loved having a place to retie their saris in private.

Another design that emerged from these particular How Might We's was increased visibility of the cleaning process. From the cleanliness-focused question, the team designed a system next to the entrance that would notify users not just when the eToilet was occupied but also when a cleaning session was in process. By allowing customers to visualize a cleaning between each use, they began to associate the toilet with a strong sense of cleanliness.

Create How Might We Questions

Turn Your Insights Into How Might We Questions

Insight:

Women want a private space in which to enter and exit the toilet.

How might we create a private zone for women before they fully exit the toilet?

Insight:

Without proper maintenance, toilets will become dirty very quickly.

How might we design toilets to be easily serviced and maintained?

Insight:

The people who live and work near a public toilet play a crucial role in directing users toward or away from it.

How might we create an experience that will drive the surrounding community to encourage more use?

Segmentation

One of the most difficult aspects of human-centered design is synthesizing everything that you've learned. Because our teams hear from so many people and collect so many interesting stories, it's easy to feel overwhelmed by information. But there are tricks you can use to get your head around what you've learned, one of which is creating frameworks. Though not every framework works for every project, you'll find that certain ones may be useful in helping you identify patterns. An IDEO.org team working on understanding post-harvest loss among farmers in Sub-Saharan Africa designed one that ended up informing their entire project.

After talking with smallholder farmers across Kenya and Senegal, the team came to realize that although they were meeting farmers in similar situations, they often had vastly different capacities, comfort with risk, and abilities to innovate.

The team looked at all their interviews and decided to do a behavioral mapping exercise in which they plotted them along a spectrum of economic stability. Those who lived on the edge were on one side of the spectrum and those with a bit of a cushion and the ability to take out a loan or experiment with a new crop were at the other end. At first they broke the smallholder farmers they met into seven different categories, but after a bit of refinement, they were able to group them in only three—Stable Farmers, Transitional Farmers, and Unstable Farmers. The team represented this trio of smallholder types with a pyramid, a framework and image that swiftly expressed the team's research.

"Pockets formed as we created the seven different segments," says business designer Shalu Umapathy, "but only after we were able to distill it down to just three categories of farmers did we realize, wow, this is really powerful."

By building a framework that helped them realize that not all smallholders are created equal, the team was able to deliver its partner, Rockefeller Foundation, a vision of how it might better intervene on their behalf. And it was a perfect example of how building a framework can unlock a new way of understanding the problem at hand.

Create Frameworks

A framework is a visual representation of a system and a great way to make sense of data. Use them to highlight key relationships and develop your strategy.

During the Ideation phase it can feel like you've got tons of information but no way to organize it. At IDEO.org, we Create Frameworks to help synthesize our learnings and find clarity in what are often highly complex challenges. Frameworks like 2x2s, relational maps, and journey maps help you start to visualize patterns, understand the perspectives of the people you're designing for, and help you unpack the context you're working in.

STEPS

TIME
60-90 minutes

DIFFICULTY
Hard

WHAT YOU'LL NEED
Pens, Post-its, paper

PARTICIPANTS
Design team

01 | As you Share Inspiring Stories (p. 78), listen for moments when the topic seems to fit into a larger system or feels related to something else you heard.

02 | When patterns start to emerge, draw them. At first they can be simple frameworks like Venn diagrams or 2x2 matrices. These simple diagrams can help you map a few forces at work at once.

03 | As the systems you hear about become more complex, and you start to think about what you might design, your frameworks will too. For example, a journey map—which charts the steps from first hearing of your product to trying it to recommending it to a friend—might become relevant.

04 | Keep refining your frameworks as you move through the Ideation phase and feel free to invent new ones. Your frameworks are bound to change, and that's OK. Frameworks are only meant to help you visualize your system, not to capture it perfectly the first time out.

Create Frameworks

Journey Map

A journey map, allows you to visualize a process beginning to end. This simple framework will help you to more easily imagine the entire flow of an experience, whether it's how a service may work or all the touchpoints of a customer's journey with a product. This doesn't need to be an in-depth, detailed representation, but rather a quick-and-dirty way of thinking out how a process unfolds.

Relational Map

A relational map is used to see how different ideas relate to one another. This type of framework can organize some of what you've learned during the Inspiration phase, visualize how things connect, and help you to find patterns. You might start by putting one idea at the center and then mapping how your other ideas and insights play off of it.

2x2

A 2x2 gives you a way to plot your ideas along two separate axes and then home in on insights and themes. By sorting information in this way, you'll uncover patterns that allow you to draw broader inferences. For instance, you might sort things based on different behavioral, societal, or environmental classifications, using each end of the axis as the extreme. If you were looking into behavioral characteristics associated with the use of adopting a new technology, the x-axis might read risk-taking versus risk-averse, while the y-axis could be digital versus analog.

Types of Frameworks

Journey Map

Relational Map

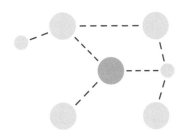

2x2

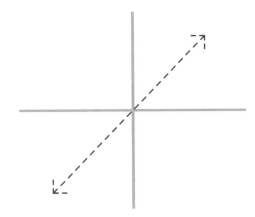

METHOD IN ACTION

Create Frameworks

In an effort to improve healthcare for informal urban workers, IDEO.org partnered with the Rockefeller Foundation and embarked on a project to identify behaviors, opportunities, and insights about their lives and circumstances.

The informal economy underpins the lives of many cities around the globe and informal workers provide services like manufacturing, domestic work, construction, waste picking, street vending, and many others. Unlike formal workers, informal workers are often exempt from any healthcare benefits or worker health standards set by the government.

So the IDEO.org team set out to better understand behaviors of informal workers, their perspectives toward health, and what influences their decision-making when it comes to health-related concerns. By more deeply understanding the emotional, spiritual, and physical realities of informal workers, the team was able to effectively identify opportunity areas and brainstorm potential healthcare interventions.

Following dozens of in-depth interviews across four countries—Kenya, South Africa, Thailand, and the Philippines—the team used 2x2 frameworks to help them sort through what they heard from people and to identify key insights. For instance, by mapping levels of disposable income across various axes, such as strength of their support network, they uncovered incredibly useful findings. These frameworks allowed them to visualize patterns in the informal workforce that could be articulated in segments. Segmentation then helped them to better define characteristics of the people they were designing for and create opportunities for design around each group. This particular 2x2 identified the Caretakers—those who have some level of disposable income and go out of their way to care for those around them— and the Survivors—those who are living day-to-day with little or no support.

In addition to the example used on the following page, the team mapped out a number of variables relating to time, financial stability, work segmentations, access to technology, and societal factors. A 2x2 is an incredibly flexible type of framework, so don't feel constrained to these examples. Change what the two axes represent until you find the 2x2 that's right for your challenge.

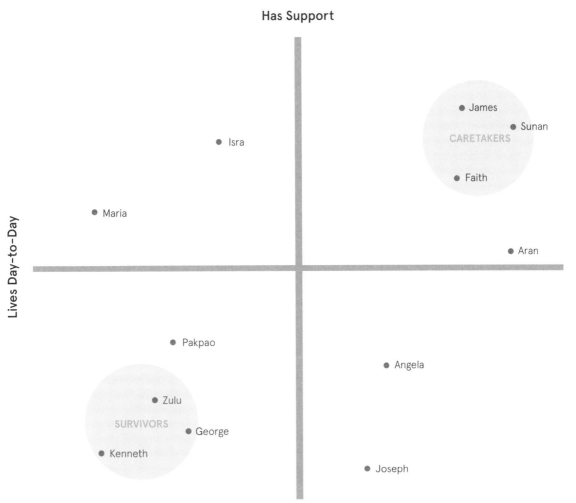

Has Support

Doesn't Have Support

Lives Day-to-Day

Has Disposable Income

- Isra
- Maria
- James
- Sunan
CARETAKERS
- Faith
- Aran
- Pakpao
- Angela
- Zulu
SURVIVORS
- George
- Kenneth
- Joseph

Brainstorm

Energize your team and drum up a staggering amount of innovative ideas.

At IDEO.org, we use Brainstorms to tap into a broad body of knowledge and creativity. Over the course of your project you should do them not only with your design team, but also with partners and the people you're designing for. Refer to Brainstorm Rules (p. 95) for the specifics of what makes for a fruitful brainstorm, but remember that the best policy is to promote openness, lots of ideas, and creativity over immediate feasibility. Brainstorms work best when the group is positive, optimistic, and focused on generating as many ideas as possible.

STEPS

TIME
30-60 minutes

DIFFICULTY
Moderate

WHAT YOU'LL NEED
Pens, Post-its, a large sheet of paper or whiteboard

PARTICIPANTS
Design team, partners, community members

01 | Pass out pens and Post-its to everyone and have a large piece of paper, wall, or whiteboard on which to stick them.

02 | Review the Brainstorm Rules before you start.

03 | Pose the question or prompt you want the group to answer. Even better if you write it down and put it at the top of the paper, wall, or whiteboard.

04 | As each person has an idea, have her describe to the group as she puts her Post-it on the wall or board.

05 | Generate as many ideas as possible.

Brainstorm Rules

At IDEO.org we have seven little rules that unlock the creative power of a brainstorming session.

We've all been in Brainstorms (p. 94) that went nowhere. At IDEO.org, the goal isn't a perfect idea, it's lots of ideas, collaboration, and openness to wild solutions. The last thing you want in a Brainstorm is someone who, instead of coming up with ideas, only talks about why the ones already mentioned won't work. Not only does that kill creativity, but it shifts the group's mindset from a generative one to a critical one. The only way to get to good ideas is to have lots to choose from.

TIME
5 minutes for review before a Brainstorm

DIFFICULTY
Easy

WHAT YOU'LL NEED
Print out the Brainstorm Rules

PARTICIPANTS
Design team, any partners or people you're designing for who are relevant

STEPS

01 | **Defer judgement.** You never know where a good idea is going to come from. The key is to make everyone feel like they can say the idea on their mind and allow others to build on it.

02 | **Encourage wild ideas.** Wild ideas can often give rise to creative leaps. When devising ideas that are wacky or out there, we tend to imagine what we want without the constraints of technology or materials.

03 | **Build on the ideas of others.** Being positive and building on the ideas of others take some skill. In conversation, we try to use " yes, and..." instead of "but."

04 | **Stay focused on the topic.** Try to keep the discussion on target, otherwise you may diverge beyond the scope of what you're trying to design for.

05 | **One conversation at a time.** Your team is far more likely to build on an idea and make a creative leap if everyone is paying full attention.

06 | **Be visual.** In Brainstorms we put our ideas on Post-its and then put them on a wall. Nothing gets an idea across faster than a sketch.

07 | **Go for quantity.** Aim for as many new ideas as possible. In a good session, up to 100 ideas are generated in 60 minutes. Crank the ideas out quickly and build on the best ones.

Bundle Ideas

Now that you've got lots of ideas, it's time to combine them into robust solutions.

Bundling Ideas takes you from strong individual concepts to solutions of substance. Think of it as a game of mix and match, with the end goal of putting the best parts of several ideas together to create more complex concepts. You've probably noticed that many ideas start to resemble each other—which is a good thing. Try different combinations; keep the best parts of some, get rid of the ones that aren't working, and consolidate your thinking into a few concepts you can start to share.

STEPS

TIME
60-90 minutes

DIFFICULTY
Hard

WHAT YOU'LL NEED
Pens, Post-its, boards

PARTICIPANTS
Design team

01 | You've got lots of drawings and ideas up on the wall, so now it's time to start moving them around and forming them into more complex solutions.

02 | Start by clustering similar ideas into groups. Talk about the best elements of those clusters and combine them with other clusters.

03 | Now, start building groupings out of the themes and patterns you've found. Focus on translating what you've heard into practice, rather than just identifying similar ideas.

04 | Once you've got a few idea groupings, ask yourself how the best elements of your thinking might live in a system. Now you're moving from individual ideas to full-on solutions!

METHOD IN ACTION

Bundle Ideas

While designing the service that would ultimately become the Nairobi water business, SmartLife, an IDEO.org design team came up with lots of ideas as to how it might work. But not until it bundled them, tossing out a few, and determining which played nicely together, was it able to arrive at a robust social enterprise.

Over the course of the Ideation phase, the team had a bunch of ideas. They heard that a catalog of products might make sense. They toyed around with a retail outlet, a subscription service, and a brand that revolved around aspirational health.

Though each of these was a fine idea alone, the true promise of SmartLife wasn't obvious until the team started bundling them. By combining the subscription service idea with a retail space with the aspirational health brand, the team solved how people could both get cumbersome cans of water delivered to their homes while still giving them a reason to come shop for products at a branded kiosk.

When you Bundle Ideas, feel free to mix and match. It may take a variety of combinations before you get a system that totally works. Also remember that though you may lead with a few ideas that are most desirable to the community you're designing for, you may need to come up with a few more ideas that fill in the logistical gaps.

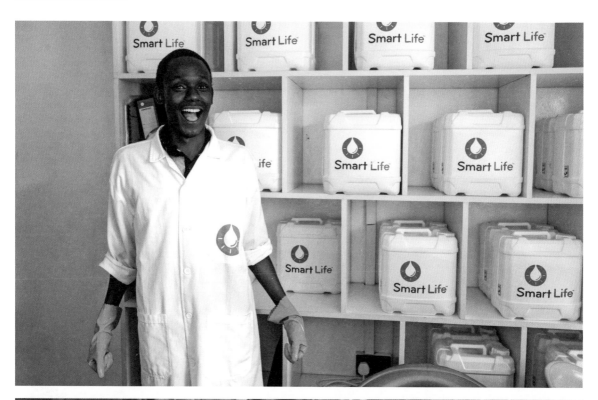

By bundling a retail outlet (top) and a delivery service (bottom), an IDEO.org team came up with the SmartLife service.

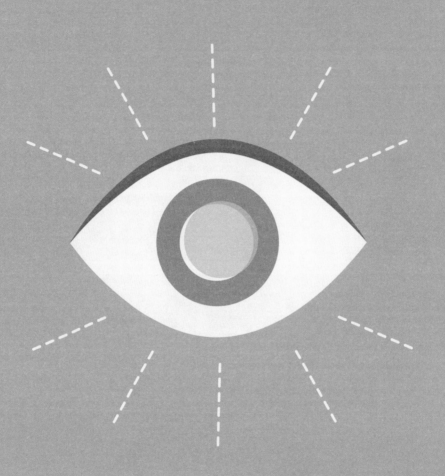

Get Visual

Incorporating drawing, sculpting, and building into the Ideation phase can unlock all kinds of innovative solutions.

A typical IDEO.org Brainstorm (p. 94) or synthesis session is a flurry of charts, drawings, cartoons, and words. Even though some people are naturally more visual and will express themselves easily through pictures, everyone can benefit from thinking visually. Getting visual makes ideas more tangible, and helps clarify your thoughts for your team. Even a super low-resolution drawing of an idea will help others understand and build upon it. And don't limit your visual thinking to just pictures. Sculpt, build, or Collage (p. 61)— anything that helps get your ideas out!

STEPS

TIME
Throughout the entire process

DIFFICULTY
Easy

WHAT YOU'LL NEED
Pen, paper, notebook, art supplies

PARTICIPANTS
Design team

01 | This is more of a general approach than a one-off activity, so always keep Post-its, paper, and pens handy in case the urge strikes to draw, graph, chart, or make.

02 | Drawings may need a bit of additional explanation, so take time to talk through your visuals with the team.

03 | If you're having trouble explaining an idea, consider drawing it. You'll be surprised at how quickly it comes into focus.

METHOD IN ACTION

Get Visual

An IDEO.org team was working in Senegal with the Rockefeller Foundation to understand how and why farmers' food spoils before it gets to market. As we talked to more and more farmers about their food spoilage problems, there came a point where we had trouble understanding just how much of their crop goes to waste, in part, perhaps, because we were framing things in terms of percentages. We'd talked through it a few times but wondered if there were another way to learn.

Our goal was to understand what portion of the farmers' crops went to market, what went to feed them and their families, and what spoils. So we put a mound of beans in a pile and asked one farmer to group them into smaller stacks to represent how much of the harvest is consumed by his family, how much is sold, and how much spoils.

Though we got a great visualization of what percentage of crops spoil, we also learned that there was one category that we didn't even know about: crops that go to the neighbors. Not only did this give us an additional data point, but also made us realize that there's an informal sharing system amongst farmers in many Senegalese villages. This prompted all kinds of additional questions about how communities band together and what post-harvest crop loss might mean at a community level as well as an individual one.

Visualizing where this farmer's crops go helped an IDEO.org team grasp what spoils and what gets to market.

Mash-Ups

What would the Harvard of agricultural extension services look like? Mash up two existing brands or concepts to explore new ideas.

Mash-Ups are similar to Analogous Inspiration (p. 53) in that each Method relies on isolating the exact quality you're looking to design into your solution. For Mash-Ups, however, this is more of a thought exercise, a chance to pose bold, even unreasonable questions to speed your thinking. If you're designing a healthful school lunch, you might ask, "What's the farmer's market version of a cafeteria?" Or if you want to make financial services more social, you might ask "What's the Facebook version of a savings account?" The trick is to layer a real-world example of the quality you need onto your design.

STEPS

TIME
30-45 minutes

DIFFICULTY
Hard

WHAT YOU'LL NEED
Pens, Post-its, paper

PARTICIPANTS
Design team

01 | The first, and hardest, part of Mash-Ups is to isolate the quality that you're looking to add to your solution. Is it efficiency, speed, cleanliness, glamour? Write it down on a Post-it and put it on the wall.

02 | Now that you've got the quality you're after, Brainstorm (p. 94) real-world examples of businesses, brands, and services that embody that quality.

03 | Now, layer that brand on top of your challenge and ask your Mash-Up question.

04 | Take your Mash-Up question and Brainstorm what it would look like in the context in which you're designing. Capture all your ideas on Post-its and put them up on the wall.

Design Principles

As you build out your ideas, you'll notice that certain unifying elements are starting to guide the design. Here's how to recognize them.

Design Principles are the guardrails of your solution—quick, memorable recipes that will help keep further iterations consistent. These principles describe the most important elements of your solution and give integrity and form to what you're designing. Odds are, they will align with the themes you found earlier in the Ideation phase. You'll also find that they'll evolve as you design things, so don't be afraid to revise them. Keep them short and memorable, like, "Talk like people talk" or "Keep women at the center of the business." Lower-level ideas like "The logo is blue" are not Design Principles.

STEPS

TIME
60-90 minutes

DIFFICULTY
Moderate

WHAT YOU'LL NEED
Pens, Post-its, themes

PARTICIPANTS
Design team

01 Look at your most important Post-its and what you came to in Finding Themes (p. 80) in particular.

02 Consider the core principles underpinning those themes. Frame these as positive statements that might tell you how and what to design. Remember, Design Principles operate as a group, and it's likely that you'll need to identify several.

03 Look at the Design Principles you've come up with. Are they short and to the point? Do they describe just one idea? Try to avoid overly complicating them. If it feels like there are multiple ideas going on, break them into smaller parts.

04 Review your Design Principles and make sure they cover the key aspects of your solution. Modify any that don't.

05 Be ready to revise your Design Principles as you start to build prototypes and test your ideas. Some Design Principles won't reveal themselves until you've actually designed and tested something, but once you spot them they'll become essential.

METHOD IN ACTION

Design Principles

"No matter what we create, from service to product to experience...our design will be relevant when we stay true to these seven Design Principles," declared an IDEO.org team working with the Bezos Family Foundation on a campaign to encourage low-income parents to engage early and often with their children. Born from the insights the team came to while conducting and synthesizing its research, these seven Design Principles served as the underlying ethos of the project, and a roadmap to how it should look, feel, and behave.

Notice how the seven principles themselves are top-level dictums, not the fine print. These principles set the tone, voice, and approach of the campaign and instruct anyone iterating on or adding to it what their work should look like.

When making your own Design Principles, try to boil them down to the essentials. They should feel like the most elemental operating instructions of your product or service. Have a look at the principles from our brain building campaign on the next page for inspiration.

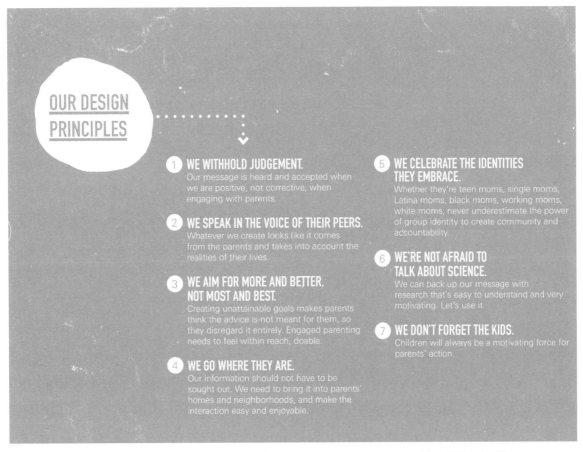

OUR DESIGN PRINCIPLES

1 WE WITHHOLD JUDGEMENT.
Our message is heard and accepted when we are positive, not corrective, when engaging with parents.

2 WE SPEAK IN THE VOICE OF THEIR PEERS.
Whatever we create looks like it comes from the parents and takes into account the realities of their lives.

3 WE AIM FOR MORE AND BETTER, NOT MOST AND BEST.
Creating unattainable goals makes parents think the advice is not meant for them, so they disregard it entirely. Engaged parenting needs to feel within reach, doable.

4 WE GO WHERE THEY ARE.
Our information should not have to be sought out. We need to bring it into parents' homes and neighborhoods, and make the interaction easy and enjoyable.

5 WE CELEBRATE THE IDENTITIES THEY EMBRACE.
Whether they're teen moms, single moms, Latina moms, black moms, working moms, white moms, never underestimate the power of group identity to create community and accountability.

6 WE'RE NOT AFRAID TO TALK ABOUT SCIENCE.
We can back up our message with research that's easy to understand and very motivating. Let's use it.

7 WE DON'T FORGET THE KIDS.
Children will always be a motivating force for parents' action.

These Design Principles show how a communication campaign to encourage parents to engage with their kids should operate.

Create a Concept

Move from a handful of ideas and insights into a fully-fledged concept, one that you'll refine and push forward.

So far you've come up with, shared, and even discarded scores of ideas. You further refined things as you Bundled Ideas (p. 97) and now it's time to turn them into a concept. A concept is more polished and complete than an idea. It's more sophisticated, something that you'll want to test with the people you're designing for, and it's starting to look like an answer to your design challenge. This is the moment where you move from problem to solution and it drives everything that comes next.

STEPS

TIME
60-90 minutes

DIFFICULTY
Hard

WHAT YOU'LL NEED
Pens, Post-its, paper

PARTICIPANTS
Design team

01 | Take the ideas that you bundled and put them up on the wall on Post-its.

02 | Now might be a good time to Create Frameworks (p. 89) out of those bundled ideas. Start to visualize where your bundles are pointing, but think especially hard about making them into a system.

03 | Don't worry too much about all the details of your solution now—you don't need a finely tuned Funding Strategy (p. 145) just yet. The goal is to get a robust, flexible concept that addresses the problem you're trying to solve.

04 | Keep referring back to your design challenge. Are you answering it? Are there elements missing in your solution? What else can you incorporate to come up with a great solution?

05 | Like the rest of human-centered design, there's a bit of trial and error here. And creating a concept means you'll probably create a couple that don't work out. That's fine.

Co-Creation Session

The people you're designing for can tell you plenty, and they can show you more. Here's how to further incorporate them into your design process.

You'll be talking with scores of people throughout your project, and a Co-Creation Session is a great way to get feedback on your ideas and bring people deeper into the process. The purpose of a Co-Creation Session is to convene a group of people from the community you're serving and then get them to design alongside you. You're not just hearing their voices, you're empowering them to join the team. You can co-create services, investigate how communities work, or understand how to brand your solution.

TIME
1-3 hours

DIFFICULTY
Moderate

WHAT YOU'LL NEED
Pens, Post-its, paper, a place to meet

PARTICIPANTS
Design team, community members, partners

STEPS

01 | The first step is to identify who you want in your Co-Creation Session. Perhaps it's a handful of people you've already interviewed. Maybe it's a particular demographic like teens or female farmers or people without jobs.

02 | Once you know who you want, arrange a space, get the necessary supplies (often pens, Post-its, paper, art supplies), and invite them to join.

03 | Maximize a Co-Creation Session with Conversation Starters (p. 45), a Brainstorm (p. 94), Role Playing (p. 118), Rapid Prototyping (p. 119), or other activities to get your group engaged.

04 | Capture the feedback your group gives you. The goal isn't just to hear from people, it's to get them on your team. Make sure that you're treating your co-creators as designers, not as Interview (p. 39) subjects.

Gut Check

You've been generating a ton of ideas. Here's a chance to look at them critically and figure out what to pursue, what to evolve, and what to discard.

The Ideation phase is about coming up with as many innovative ideas as possible, often with less emphasis on plausibility or implementation. At IDEO.org, this approach certainly leads to more creative thinking, but we also know that some of our more far-out ideas are probably better left on the drawing board. This Gut Check exercise can help you look at your ideas through a more critical lens and help you decide which ideas truly merit your efforts.

STEPS

TIME
30-60 minutes

DIFFICULTY
Moderate

WHAT YOU'LL NEED
Pens, paper

PARTICIPANTS
Design team

01 | Have a look at your most promising ideas and try to distill them down to their essences. For example, if your idea is about redesigning the patient experience in a health clinic, the core idea might be achieving more patient privacy.

02 | Now, list all the constraints and barriers that stand in your way. Put them on Post-its and display them for everyone to see. Don't feel daunted if the list is long. Constraints make for great design!

03 | This might be a great time to have a quick Brainstorm (p. 94) about how to evolve your idea within the constraints you just listed. How can you keep the core of your idea but push it so that it remains within your capabilities?

04 | Don't be afraid of letting an idea go. The Gut Check is here to help you make the most promising ideas real.

Determine What to Prototype

There are so many ways to prototype an idea.
Here's how to isolate what to test.

Your idea will have lots of testable components, so be clear about what you need to learn and which components will give you the necessary answers. Prototyping isn't about being precious. Make simple, scrappy prototypes to not only save time, but to focus on testing just the critical elements. You might be trying to learn something like, "How big should this be?" or "What should the uniforms of the social enterprise look like?" At this stage you should have a lot of questions about how your idea should work. This is a great way to begin answering them.

STEPS

TIME
30 minutes

DIFFICULTY
Moderate

WHAT YOU'LL NEED
Pens, Post-its, paper

PARTICIPANTS
Design team

01 | With your team, write down the key elements of your idea. Think practically about what needs to be tested and write down your primary questions for each component.

02 | Now pick a few questions to answer. If you want to prototype an interaction, consider putting on a skit with your team. If you're testing a logo, print it out and stick it on a t-shirt to solicit feedback.

03 | Think through what kind of prototype makes the most sense to answer these questions. You might consider holding a Brainstorm (p. 94) now.

04 | Remember, this process is about learning, not getting it right the first time. Better to test a miserable failure and learn from it, rather than take ages making a beautiful, highly refined prototype.

Prototyping and Iteration

A hallmark of human-centered design is rapid prototyping and iterating on the fly. A project team working in Ethiopia on designing a new device to plant teff—a grain and staple of Ethiopian cuisine—put our process to the test when a prototype of their planter came face to face with the Ethiopian soil.

Transporting the planter from San Francisco to rural Ethiopia was one thing, but the real challenge came when engineer and team member Ravi Prakash set out to push it through a field of muddy soil.

"Suddenly, Ravi's steps started getting smaller. Watching him was like seeing time slow down," reported project lead Martin Schnitzer. "He was barely 50 feet down the field and the wheels had picked up enough mud to make it nearly impossible to move any further. We knew the mud would be challenging but we didn't think it would render the planter useless so quickly. Deflated, we felt like we were thrown back to the beginning of our challenge."

The team was quickly back in the shop of a local agricultural research center trying to figure out what to do with the planter's wheels. They played with a variety of solutions, quickly moving through ideas like spiked wheels and skis, until one of the local metal workers had a suggestion: wrap the wheels in burlap.

"Wrapping the wheels in burlap isn't an idea we could have ever come up with in a brainstorm," said Schnitzer, "and burlap certainly isn't on any list of new high tech materials. However, using burlap came from keeping an open mind to trying new solutions. It came from talking to people who understand the conditions best and by sharing the excitement of this project with others to gain inspiration from a number of places."

In the end, burlap worked wonderfully well. And though the wheels of the final product are made of harder-wearing stuff, the burlap fix allowed the team to get back out into the soil and test other elements of the planters with the farmers who'll use them.

Storyboard

A quick, low-resolution prototype, Storyboards can help you visualize your concept from start to finish.

You don't need to be a great artist to create a great Storyboard. By visually plotting out elements of your product or service, you can learn a lot about your idea. Not only will this method help you refine what your idea is, it can also help you understand who will use it, where, and how. Like all prototypes, the idea here is to make something really rough as a way to help you think the idea through. It's amazing what putting pen to paper can reveal.

STEPS

TIME
60 minutes

DIFFICULTY
Easy

WHAT YOU'LL NEED
Pens, Storyboard worksheets p. 178

PARTICIPANTS
Design team

01 | Determine what part of your idea you want to Storyboard. You don't have to Storyboard the entire thing, and you may find it useful to test a component of your idea like an interaction, or how a customer finds out about your product.

02 | Spend no more than 30-45 minutes drawing how your ideas work. Use the series of comic book-style frames on p. 178 or make your own. This will help you spotlight key moments and build a short narrative.

03 | Don't get hung up on your drawing abilities. It's more important that a Storyboard helps you fully think through your concept than create something that looks beautiful.

04 | Once you're done, act out the Storyboard to your team for feedback.

METHOD IN ACTION

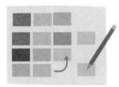

Storyboard

An IDEO.org team, working to help victims of Typhoon Yolanda in the Philippines rebuild their financial lives, made excellent use of Storyboards. The team was working with international relief organization Mercy Corps and the bank BanKO to come up with a loan product that would help people get back on their feet and give them access to increasing amounts of credit. In addition to offering credit, one of the novel elements of the loan product—named a PabilinKO loan—was that it would incorporate a fund to pay for a person's burial costs.

A Storyboard was the perfect tool to show how a customer would learn about the loan, the actions she would need to take to get it, and how it would impact her life.

By drawing and describing a handful of points along the way, the team was able to visualize how someone would use a PabilinKO loan, the benefits it offers, and the process of getting one and paying it back.

Use the Storyboard template on p. 178 to make your own. And remember that artistic skill isn't necessary. The idea is to think through the steps in a process, not to create an artistic masterpiece. Stick figures are just fine so long as they can convey what's supposed to happen each step of the way.

Storyboard

Title _Meet Paulita_

What's Happening

Paulita has two children, Roberta and Felipe.
Her house was destroyed in the typhoon. She
is a beneficiary of Mercy Corps and she needs
a loan to rebuild her cleaning business. She's
heard that PabilinKO is easy to get and that it
will help her get back on her feet.

Title _Paulita Signs Up_

What's Happening

Paulita travels to the local market and stops
by the PabilinKO stall. She gives her Barangay
papers and ID to the agent, and just like that
he can sign her up for her first loan. Paulita
receives a text confirming that she's officially a
PabilinKO customer!

Storyboard

Title She Cashes Out

What's Happening

Paulita goes to the nearest BanKO Partner Outlet (BPO), which is conveniently located in the same market. With her phone number and ID, she "cashes out" and takes her money with her.

Title She Makes a Payment

I'd like to pay 100P on my loan please.

What's Happening

Back in the village, Paulita goes to an agent to pay her weekly installments. This is great for her because the nearest BPO is 10 kilometers away, and she cannot visit often. Paulita pays, and the agent sends that money to BanKO. Paulita receives a text confirming that this installment was paid.

Storyboard

Title <u>11 Weeks Later...</u>

What's Happening

<u>Paulita makes her final loan payment. She's</u>
<u>proud to have built up her cleaning business</u>
<u>with the help of BanKO. She receives a</u>
<u>congratulatory text that tells her the pabilin</u>
<u>burial fund is now hers and it comes with 100P</u>
<u>to get started. Because Paulita successfully</u>
<u>paid her first PabilinKO loan, she has the option</u>
<u>of taking a second, larger one.</u>

Title <u>Paulita Grows Her Fund</u>

What's Happening

<u>Paulita can continue to grow her pabilin fund</u>
<u>anytime she has some extra cash. For example,</u>
<u>at the sale of her pig, after a great week of</u>
<u>business, or when her daughter sends her</u>
<u>remittances from Manila.</u>

Role Playing

A quick and tangible way to test an idea or experience is to get into character and act it out.

Role Playing is a type of prototype that is not only pretty easy to build, but can also help you get an idea, experience, or product in front of the people you're designing for quickly. You'd be smart to try Role Playing with your design team first. You may learn a lot by trying on the roles of the people in your small skit before you even get out of the office.

STEPS

TIME
30-45 minutes

DIFFICULTY
Moderate

WHAT YOU'LL NEED
Costumes help, but aren't entirely necessary

PARTICIPANTS
Design team, people you're designing for

01 The main goal of prototyping is to make an idea just tangible enough to elicit a response, whether from you, your team, a partner, or whomever you're designing for.

02 Decide which of your ideas you want to Role Play and assign the necessary roles to your team members.

03 Take about 30 minutes to determine the necessary roles, who will play them, and what it is that you're looking to test—is it a type of interaction, whether a person will respond to a type of product, the effectiveness of a sales pitch?

04 Costumes and props can be highly effective tools in bringing your Role Play to life. Don't spend ages on them, but consider making your prototype that much more realistic. You'd be surprised how far just a few details can go toward making a Role Play feel real.

Rapid Prototyping

Build your prototypes quickly, share them immediately, and keep on learning.

For human-centered designers, Rapid Prototyping is an incredibly effective way to make ideas tangible, to learn through making, and to quickly get key feedback from the people you're designing for. Because prototypes are meant only to convey an idea—not to be perfect—you can quickly move through a variety of iterations, building on what you've learned from the people you're designing for. Rapid Prototyping means that you're building only enough to test your idea, and that you're right back in there making it better once you've gotten feedback.

STEPS

TIME
120 minutes

DIFFICULTY
Hard

WHAT YOU'LL NEED
Pen, paper, supplies

PARTICIPANTS
Design team

01 Once you've Determined What to Prototype (p. 111), it's time to build it.

02 You can make any number of prototypes: Storyboards (p. 113), Role Playing (p. 118), models, mock-ups. The goal here it to make something tangible that conveys the idea you want to test. No need to make it perfect, just make it good enough to get the idea across.

03 Now take your prototype out and test it with people you're designing for. Put it in their hands and ask them what they make of it. Make sure to Get Feedback (p. 126).

04 Here is where you can Integrate Feedback and Iterate (p. 127). Once you've quickly built another prototype you'll do it all over again until it's just right.

METHOD IN ACTION

Rapid Prototype

While working with Juhudi Kilimo in Kenya, Rapid Prototyping was key to an IDEO.org team finding out how to best disburse technical agricultural information to local farmers.

Juhudi Kilimo is a social enterprise in Kenya that provides asset financing for agricultural equipment, agricultural insurance, and training on new farming technologies. They brought on IDEO.org to design new ways of providing agricultural training to farmers. After several weeks of field research, the team uncovered a number of different insights about smallholder farmers. Among others, a few key findings showed that farmers trust expertise and experience but often don't have access to unbiased information. Additionally, peer-to-peer learning is one of the best agents for changing farming practices.

To test whether these insights could guide a new service, the team made two prototypes. First they created a short video featuring a local farmer, Isaac, and his success in growing his chicken business. At the end of the screening, they gave out a call center telephone number where farmers could call in with questions and talk to an agricultural expert. To build this as a rough prototype—without building a whole call center— the team compiled questions that came in over the course of a week with call back numbers. Then, they hired an agriculturist to come in for just one

day to return the calls and answer the questions. This was a quick way to validate a couple key questions: a) would these videos resonate with farmers and inspire them to seek agricultural training to better their own farms; and b) would a call center be an effective way of disbursing this technical information?

Turns out, the call center wasn't an ideal outcome, but it did validate the idea that expertise was important. In the end, the design team changed course and made videos to educate farmers about new practices. But it wouldn't have gotten there if at first it didn't prototype the call center and learn more about the best way to communicate with farmers.

When you prototype, you can make almost anything. Don't be discouraged if what you make isn't a hit. As long as you're learning, it's not true failure.

By creating a short video (top) and prototyping a simple call center (bottom), this team learned what works and what doesn't when it comes to providing agricultural training in Kenya.

Business Model Canvas

This handy worksheet can help you think through some key aspects of a social enterprise, service, or business.

As you solidify your idea and start to test it, you'll also need to remain cognizant of your business model. A good way to keep it front and center in your mind is by using a Business Model Canvas. This simple sheet asks you key questions like what's your revenue stream, what are key partnerships you'll need to forge, and what resources are vital to your operation. You might even use a Business Model Canvas several times in the process as elements are bound to change as you refine your idea and move toward implementing it.

STEPS

TIME
90 minutes

DIFFICULTY
Moderate

WHAT YOU'LL NEED
Pens, Business Model Canvas
worksheet p. 180

PARTICIPANTS
Design team

01 | Print out a Business Model Canvas for each of your team members. There's a good one in the Resources section on p. 180.

02 | Sit down with your team and start to fill out the sections of the Business Model Canvas. When you fill it out the first time, expect for there to be holes. It's okay not to know exactly how everything will work.

03 | You may need to pause filling out the sheet to get more information.

04 | When you're done, post the Business Model Canvas in your workspace. Like everything else in the human-centered design process, you'll refine it. Consider doing a new one as your project progresses.

METHOD IN ACTION

Business Model Canvas

Partnering with Water and Sanitation for the Urban Poor (WSUP) to improve sanitation solutions in Zambia, an IDEO.org team set out to design the brand and business model for a pit latrine emptying service.

To make sure they were leveraging a new vacuum truck technology—which allowed for more effective and efficient emptying of pit latrines—in a way that best suited the community, the designers set to work thinking about what type of business and service model should be built around it. Ultimately, the service model was designed to encompass a variety of subscription models, from monthly payments for recurring partial emptying service to one-time payments for a full service. This would allow the business to accommodate families with varying levels of liquidity. But in addition to creating a payment system that worked for the community members, the design team needed to find a viable business model for the service itself.

To get a better idea of what might work, they used a Business Model Canvas. This enabled the team to map out and understand what their business might look like from the partners and activities necessary to get the idea off the ground to the value proposition offered to the customer. Furthermore this model provided a quick way to check cost versus revenue streams, which was crucial to seeing if the concept could be taken forward as a sustainable service.

Business Model Canvas

Designed for: Partners and franchise owners/customers

Designed by: IDEO.org

Date: April, 2013   Version:

Key Partners 🔗

Maintenance provider

Franchiser/supplier

Finance

Dump site

Manual pit latrine emptiers

Key Activities ◥

Emptying

Collecting

Key Resources 🛢

Consumer-facing collateral

Pit latrine emptying technology

Value Propositions 🎁

Full service
- High tech aspirational
- Affordable
- Full empty
- Able to reach every home

Partial Service
- Partial empty
- Fits a users current spending behavior

Customer Relationships ❤

Professional service provider

Channels 🎥

- Door-to-door sales
- Kiosk
- Referrals
- Branding on trucks
- The road
- 1-800-dispatch
- Branded toilet

Customer Segments 👥

Latrine owners in urban communities

Cost Structure 🏷

- Commissions
- Equipment lease/franchise fee
- Operator/driver salary
- Gas
- Maintenance
- Dumping costs

Revenue Streams 💰

Full Service —> One-time emptying

Partial —> Monthly subscription

Strategyzer
strategyzer.com

Get Feedback

You've learned and built. Now share what you've made with the people you're designing for and see what they think.

Soliciting feedback on your ideas and prototypes is a core element of the Ideation phase, and it helps keep the people you're designing for at the center of your project. It's also a direct path to designing something that those same people will adopt. If the point of a prototype is to test an idea, then collecting feedback from potential users is what pushes things forward.

STEPS

TIME
60-90 minutes

DIFFICULTY
Moderate

WHAT YOU'LL NEED
Pens, paper, your prototype

PARTICIPANTS
Design team, people you're designing for

01 | Now that you've got a prototype to share, get it in front of the people you're designing for. There are lots of ways to do it: Reconvene a Group Interview (p. 42), intercept people in markets for Interviews (p. 39), do another Expert Interview (p. 43) with your prototype, or perhaps run a Co-Creation Session (p. 109) designed to elicit feedback.

02 | Capturing honest feedback is crucial. People may praise your prototype to be nice, so assure them that this is only a tool by which to learn and that you welcome honest, even negative feedback.

03 | Share with lots of people so that you get a variety of reactions. Refer back to Extremes and Mainstreams (p. 49) to make sure you're capturing a cross-section of potential users.

04 | Write down the feedback you hear and use this opportunity with the people you're designing for to ask more questions and push your ideas further.

Integrate Feedback and Iterate

Let the feedback of the people you're designing for guide the next iteration of your solution.

Integrating the feedback you hear from the people you're designing for is one of the essential elements of human-centered design. You learned from people in the Inspiration phase, and in the Ideation phase one of the best ways to keep learning from them is to show them what you've made and find out what they think. Integrating their feedback into your work and then coming up with another prototype is the best way to refine your idea until it's something that's bound to be adopted and embraced.

STEPS

TIME
90-120 minutes

DIFFICULTY
Hard

WHAT YOU'LL NEED
Information from Get Feedback p. 126, prototyping materials, Post-its

PARTICIPANTS
Design team

01 | Sit with your design team and share the feedback that you collected. Use the Share Inspiring Stories (p. 78) or Download Your Learnings (p. 77) Methods to share what you learned.

02 | You'll now probably want to synthesize some of the feedback you got. You can Create Frameworks (p. 89) based on what you heard and how it applies to your idea. You might also now try a Brainstorm (p. 94) around how your idea could change based on your feedback.

03 | Get tangible and start building the next iteration of your prototype. Integrating Feedback and Iterating is closely tied to Rapid Prototyping (p. 119). So once you've determined how your prototype should change to reflect the feedback you got, build it.

04 | Remember that this is a method for refining your idea, not for getting to the ultimate solution the first time. You'll probably do it a few times to work out the kinks and get to the right answer.

Case Study: Asili

Designing a sustainable community-owned health, agricultural, and water business in the Democratic Republic of the Congo.

One out of every five children don't live to their fifth birthdays in the Democratic Republic of the Congo (DRC), a country torn by years of war and extreme poverty. The American Refugee Committee (ARC) engaged IDEO.org to help design a way to get better health care to the young children of the DRC, and together we designed Asili, a sustainable business that offers agricultural services, clean water, and a health clinic to its members. By addressing an entire ecosystem of need, from potable drinking water to better seeds to vastly improved health care for children under five, IDEO.org helped ARC impact an entire community. And after an incredibly encouraging start, ARC is already thinking about how Asili might scale.

DESIGN TEAM
4 IDEO.org designers

PARTNERS
American Refugee Committee

TIMELINE
12 weeks of design from IDEO.org; time
to launch 11 months

LOCATION
Bukavu, Democratic Republic of
the Congo

THE OUTCOME

Asili launched in July 2014 and in the span of mere months had already served
a great number of people at its clinic, water point, and agricultural center.
Just a few harvest cycles in, farmers are reporting a better yield of potatoes,
peas, and beans thanks to the seeds purchased from Asili. Despite their severe
poverty, locals are buying into Asili because it works for them. Fittingly, "Asili"
means "foundation" in Swahili, and we're seeing the people of Bukavu build
on it. A restaurant, vendors, even preliminary groundwork for electricity
have cropped up near the clinic, a clear sign that designing with direct input
from a community leads to solutions that are adopted and embraced. Just as
importantly, ARC has internalized human-centered design and taken the design
principles that IDEO.org devised and brought them to life.

INSPIRATION

The key to the Inspiration phase, as is so often the case, came from immersing
in the context in which the team was designing. That meant weeks of coming
to understand the people who live there. The design team knew that of the 20
percent of children who don't see their fifth birthdays in the DRC, many die
preventable deaths from diseases like pneumonia, diarrhea, and malaria. But
before they could figure out how to get those kids the health care that they
need, they had to better understand the social dynamics around health itself.

Thanks to scores of interviews with the residents of Bukavu, the team came
to insights that would guide Asili's design. One insight came from a woman
who said that she used to seek prenatal care for her child, but she stopped
because she never knew how much it would cost. The team realized that her
child's future could be drastically improved with a little more clarity at the
clinic, and from there, they knew that transparency and reliability had to be
core to the solution.

IDEATION

Because the design team talked to lots of people, and because they knew
that they'd have to anchor the service model deeply in the community, they
decided to learn more and test some of their ideas with a co-creation session.

While conducting interviews in the Inspiration phase, the team met with dozens of people, but seven women in particular stuck out.

So the team invited them to a two-day workshop where the women joined the process and helped design the service, brainstorming a name, a logo, and more. The two days were incredibly fruitful, with the women quickly jumping into the roles of designer, prototyper, and problem solver. By inserting these community members directly into the design process itself, the team came to grasp so much more than it could have by simply interviewing them. They learned about social dynamics in Bukavu, how power should be balanced throughout the community, and how a service that treats people like consumers might have a chance at sustainability.

Armed with the desires and ideas of the community, the design team returned to San Francisco with a clear vision of how Asili should work, how it should communicate, and how it might make money. So after a few more furious weeks of designing the system, service, business, identity, and more, the design team turned an Asili roadmap over to ARC.

IMPLEMENTATION

Together with ARC, IDEO.org's design team devised a full-on sustainable business tailored to meet the realities people in the DRC face every day. It extended from a business model to a staffing structure, launch plan, and all components of the service.

As ARC set Asili in motion, bringing it to market in one of the world's poorest countries, they went far beyond the playbook that IDEO.org laid out. Instead, ARC took a human-centered approach to implementing the vision for Asili. A perfect example is how ARC continued to build on the design principle that transparency is key. Though the team designed clear signage with posted prices, ARC realized that the Asili clinic could even better serve the community if it had a patient's bill of rights. Through close collaboration with IDEO.org, ARC deeply understands how to implement, adapt, and grow Asili as it continues to build out the multi-offer service.

IMPLEMENTATION

In the Implementation phase you'll bring your solution to life, and to market. You'll build partnerships, refine your business model, pilot your idea, and eventually get it out there. And you'll know that your solution will be a success because you've kept the very people you're looking to serve at the heart of the process.

THIS PHASE WILL HELP YOU ANSWER

How do I plan for what's next?

How do I make my concept real?

How do I assess if my solution is working?

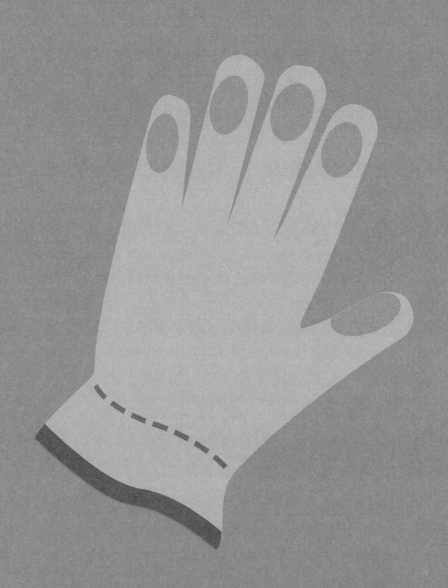

Live Prototyping

A Live Prototype is a chance to run your solution for a couple of weeks out in the real world.

Though you've been getting feedback from the people you're designing for all along, a Live Prototype is one of the most powerful ways to test your solution in the marketplace. Until now, your prototypes have been rough, and they've done only enough to convey the idea you wanted to test. A Live Prototype, however, gives you a chance to stress test your solution in real-world conditions. It can run from a few days to a few weeks, and is a chance to learn how your solution works in practice. Live Prototypes are all about understanding the feasibility and viability of your idea.

STEPS

TIME
A few days to multiple weeks

DIFFICULTY
Hard

WHAT YOU'LL NEED
Space, staff, permits, or whatever it takes to run your solution in real market conditions

PARTICIPANTS
Design team, key partners, additional staff

01 | The first thing to do is to determine what it is you want to test in your Live Prototype. It could be the way that people find out about your solution or how your service will run or how your distribution model works. For example, you could run a business out of a kiosk for a week to test a channel strategy.

02 | Once you've decided on what you're testing, sort out the logistics of your Live Prototype. Do you need a physical space, additional staff, uniforms, a permit, or anything else?

03 | If you have the capacity, think about running a few Live Prototypes at once. This will allow you to test a variety of ideas quickly, and see how they work together, which may also be important.

04 | Never stop iterating. If something went wrong on Day 1, try a new approach on Day 2. Live Prototypes are all about learning quickly, iterating on the fly, and pushing your solution closer and closer to the real thing.

05 | As always, capture feedback from the people you're designing for.

Roadmap

You'll need a timeline and a plan of action to get your idea out into the world. A Roadmap can help keep you on time and on target.

You've got a concept you feel great about and you've tested it in the world. Now you'll need to create a plan for how you're going to implement it. A Roadmap helps you gather the key stakeholders in your project and collectively figure out a timeline, assign responsibility for each element of the project, and establish milestones. This is a great Method to do alongside Resource Assessment (p. 137) and Staff Your Project (p. 144) to give you a full picture of how to build your Roadmap.

STEPS

TIME
90 minutes

DIFFICULTY
Moderate

WHAT YOU'LL NEED
Pens, Post-its, paper, calendar

PARTICIPANTS
Design team, key stakeholders, partners

01 Assemble your design team as well as all the critical stakeholders and partners responsible for implementing your idea.

02 Print out a big calendar for the next year or 18 months and use it to map out what needs to happen when. Start putting Post-its on the calendar with key dates like Pilot (p. 146) launch, go-to-market date, etc.

03 It's easy to get lost in all that needs to happen, so think about your calendar in chunks. Figure out what needs to occur in the next month, in three months, in a year. Themes will emerge around the various tracks of work that will need to take place.

04 Think about the major milestones in your project timeline—when you go to market, when you need to start manufacturing, when you launch your website—and get them on the calendar. Use a different colored Post-it for milestones—perhaps even flip them so they look like diamonds instead of squares to stand out.

05 As you add Post-its to the calendar, assign a team member or partner to each track of work. Find someone to own or champion each element of your project and prepare to hold them accountable to the tasks.

Resource Assessment

You've got a great solution, but what is it going to take to execute it? The team you've currently got may not be enough.

Devising an innovative solution and putting it into practice are two different propositions. This Method will help you understand the feasibility of your solution and where your organization will have to seek help. It makes sense to do this exercise in conjunction with Staff Your Project (p. 144) and Roadmap (p. 136). Taken as a whole, these three Methods will help point you toward the practical implementation of your work.

STEPS

TIME
60 minutes

DIFFICULTY
Easy

WHAT YOU'LL NEED
Pens, Post-its, Resource Assessment worksheet p. 182

PARTICIPANTS
Design team

01 The main elements of implementation that you'll want to understand here are the distribution of your solution, the partners you might need, and the capabilities necessary to execute. Your latest Business Model Canvas (p. 123) should have some of these answers.

02 Start to fill out the Resource Assessment worksheet on p. 182. List what you've already got and what you'll need. You may want to have a Brainstorm (p. 94) about what needs to happen for each of the main categories: Distribution, Activities, Capabilities, and Responsibilities. For example, under Distribution, perhaps you're considering selling through a storefront model and indirectly through wholesale. Fill out a Resource Assessment worksheet for each model to compare.

03 As you look at all your ideas after the Brainstorm, start to group needs based on actors in the room, and then include a category for needs that are out of the scope of the team. You can list these under Still Needed.

04 Look at how you plan to Staff Your Project. Do you need more or less help after assessing your resources?

METHOD IN ACTION

Resource Assessment

In partnership with Marie Stopes International (MSI), IDEO.org undertook a year-long engagement to design and build out a teen-specific reproductive health program in Lusaka, Zambia.

In the early stages of the project, the team immersed itself in the lives of teens to learn more about what resonates with them, what was it like to simply be a teen, and how reproductive health services could fit into their lives. They then worked closely with MSI to design a teen-friendly model for their reproductive health services which revolved around the Divine Divas, a set of characters each representing a different contraceptive method. The Divas offered a way for teens to understand and talk about contraceptives in a way that was highly relatable. From the Divas, and the design principles on which they were based, sprang a redesign of the clinic itself, branding, an outreach strategy, and a communications approach.

The team Live Prototyped this new program in a few ways. First they tried it in a cheerful teen-only space they designed called the Diva Centre. They met with success right off the bat and realized that this approach was indeed an effective way of reaching girls and getting them services. However, they were unsure if this was the most effective model to implement broadly. And so they set out to try another approach. Could the program be equally as effective but less cost- or resource-intensive if they were to try creating these teen-only spaces within existing clinics? Could pop-up clinics work?

To test this out, the design team did a few Resources Assessment worksheets to better understand what it would mean to implement the original design in new spaces and forms. By filling out Resource Assessment worksheets for each model they were considering, the team was able to compare what pieces of the puzzle they'd need for each iteration.

This exercise can be extremely helpful in not just mapping out what program implementation means in terms of the distribution, activities, capabilities, and responsibilities required, but also for identifying gaps in your thinking. It's a way of viewing the project with a lens for implementing responsibility, capacity, and staffing. On the next page see how they used this resource for the original Diva Centre concept.

Resource Assessment

Distribution	Activities	Capabilities	Responsibilities				Still Needed?
How are you getting your concept out into the world? Are there multiple ways?	What activities will be required to make your idea work?	What are we already capable of?	Design Team	Implementing Org	Funder	External	
Stand-alone Diva Centre	Physical space	Space procurement + cost			●		Community mapping
		Interior design	●	●			
		Cleaning + general maintenance		●			
	Teen outreach	Training teen connectors		●			External events through partnerships w/ local NGOs
		In-house events					
		Canvassing	●	●			
	Clinical services	Nurse consultations		●			Increased training + treatment for STIs
		Contraceptive treatment		●			
		STI testing + treatment		●			
	Non-clinical services	Data collection + entry		●			Ongoing community engagement
		Management		●			
		Cross-clinic management		●			
	Follow-ups	Pre-service call backs		●			
		Post-service call backs		●			
		Call center		●			
	Performance tracking	Data evaluation		●			Quality tracking Cost metrics + effectiveness
		Feedback loop		●			
		Data software			●		
	Informational materials	Promotional material Production	●				
		Distribution		●			
	Inventory management	Clinical supplies		●			
		Non-clinical supplies		●			
		Contraceptives		●			

Build Partnerships

You may need some help getting your concept to market. Build the partnerships you'll need now.

As you move through the Implementation phase you may realize that you'll need to rely on a variety of partners. You can identify the funding partners you'll need by using the Funding Strategy (p. 145) and Sustainable Revenue (p. 152) Methods. And you can use the Business Model Canvas (p. 123) and Resource Assessment (p. 137) to see who is necessary for getting your idea off the ground. The key idea here is to identify the partners you'll need and to build relationships with them.

STEPS

TIME
60 minutes

DIFFICULTY
Moderate

WHAT YOU'LL NEED
Pens, Post-its, paper

PARTICIPANTS
Design team, key
stakeholders, partners

01 Get your design team together with other key stakeholders and partners. Ideally these same people will or already have worked on your Roadmap (p. 136), Funding Strategy, and Sustainable Revenue.

02 Start with a Brainstorm (p. 94) around what your primary partnership needs are. Maybe you need greater access to the press, maybe you need to raise money. Determine what you need.

03 Next, take those key partnership needs and have another Brainstorm around who you know already and who you can reach out to in your greater network.

04 Though you'll want to remain flexible, you'll also want to start to set parameters around what you need from your partners. Figure out when you'll need each one, how much you can reasonably ask of them, and what kind of deadlines to set around your ask.

Ways to Grow Framework

This chart will help you understand whom your design solution is for and what implementation will look like.

The Ways to Grow Framework is a quick and visual way to understand just how difficult your design solutions might be to implement. This exercise will help you identify whether your solutions are incremental, evolutionary, or revolutionary and whether your solutions extend, adapt, or create a totally new offering. You'll also clarify whether your solutions are targeted at your current user group or whether they expand to a new group. By seeing your solutions in relation to each other, you'll quickly ascertain which ones your organization has the means, manpower, and capacity to undertake.

STEPS

TIME
30-45 minutes

DIFFICULTY
Easy

WHAT YOU'LL NEED
Pens, Post-its, Ways to Grow
Framework worksheet p. 184

PARTICIPANTS
Design team

01 Use the Ways to Grow Framework worksheet on p. 184 or draw one on a large sheet of paper. The vertical axis represents the novelty of your offering and the horizontal axis represents its users. Totally new offerings land above the horizontal axis and existing ones land below. An idea aimed at new users falls to the right of the vertical axis and one that affects existing users falls to the left.

02 Now, plot your solutions on the worksheet. Revolutionary new ideas that will attract new users will fall in the top right quadrant. Incremental ideas that offer small builds on existing services will hit below the horizontal axis.

03 Look at the distribution of solutions from incremental to revolutionary. Are there gaps in your portfolio of solutions? Are parts of the matrix blank and others full? If so, do you want to devise solutions that fill all four quadrants?

04 Lots of organizations say that they're interested in revolutionary thinking, but often, incremental and evolutionary change can have the greatest chance for big impact. Think hard about what your organization can realistically achieve and what will benefit your constituents most.

METHOD IN ACTION

Ways to Grow Framework

In-home sanitation is a huge problem in Kumasi, Ghana, and a challenge that IDEO.org, Unilever, and Water and Sanitation for the Urban Poor, sought to help remedy with the new enterprise Clean Team. Though the ultimate service, one that has gone to market and is already serving thousands of low-income Ghanaians, offers an in-home toilet and waste disposal system, it wasn't the only idea that the team entertained.

A great way to help understand how your various solutions stack up against each other, and to ascertain which ones are most feasible to implement given your capacity, try using a Ways to Grow Framework.

The Clean Team designers had three service models in mind: the high-touch system that it eventually chose, a variation on the pit latrines that are common in Ghana, and a Bag and Bin service that offered a central collection point for people to manage their waste. A Ways to Grow Framework helped them understand how each idea targeted new customers and how novel the service it offered would be to the Kumasi market.

By plotting their three models on the Ways to Grow Framework, they came to realize that the high-touch sanitation system was both most revolutionary (it was a totally new service) and was highly focused on new customers (because

few in the community had in-home toilets). The All-in-One VIP pit latrine concept was inspired by an existing offer, but targeted a new group of users. And the Bag and Bin concept landed on the upper half of the framework because it offered a new service to existing users.

In the end, the team determined that it had the capacity to enact the most revolutionary idea and the one that targeted the most new subscribers.

When you're mapping your concepts across a Ways to Grow Framework, think hard about what you can actually implement. Though it's easy to be seduced by what feels most revolutionary, you might find that more incremental innovation is easier to implement and may actually offer the biggest impact to the community you're serving.

Ways to Grow Framework

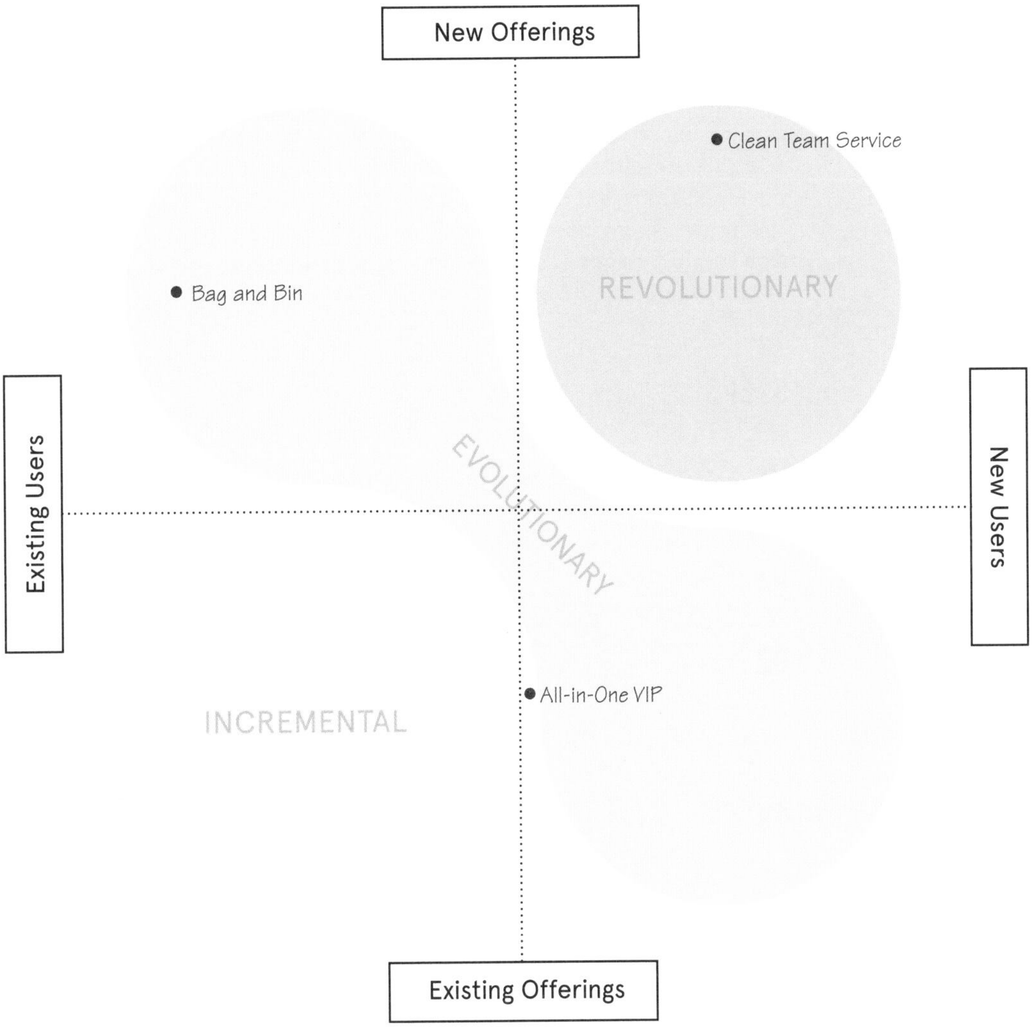

New Offerings

● Clean Team Service

REVOLUTIONARY

● Bag and Bin

EVOLUTIONARY

Existing Users

New Users

INCREMENTAL

● All-in-One VIP

Existing Offerings

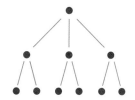

Staff Your Project

Now that you've got an idea to put in motion, build the team that can take you from concept to completion.

The methodology here is pretty similar to when you built a team in the Inspiration phase, only this time you'll want to be far more targeted. A multi-disciplinary team was great for arriving at unexpected ideas and novel solutions, but in the Implementation phase you'll be looking for specialized know-how, technical capacity, outside partners, and funding. Now might be a good time for some team members to roll off your project and others to roll on.

STEPS

TIME
60 minutes

DIFFICULTY
Hard

WHAT YOU'LL NEED
Pens, paper

PARTICIPANTS
Design team, key partners

01 Now that you're most of the way through your project, determine who are the most essential members of your team for the Implementation phase. Make a list of the most important skills that are required by team members for successful implementation. Then reorder the list based on highest priority.

02 Take a look at your existing team. If your team has shrunk, do you need to replace anyone? Do you need a special skill at this point, perhaps a business designer, someone with manufacturing expertise, a healthcare expert?

03 Do you need a project manager now that the Inspiration and Ideation phases are over?

04 Are there organizations that you now need to partner with? What about funders? Will you have to get buy-in from managers or officials to implement your idea?

05 Implementation can take a long time, so think down the road about who you'll need now and who you'll need when you get to market.

Funding Strategy

Without a coherent Funding Strategy in place, you may not have the money you need to get your design solution off the ground.

A Funding Strategy will get you the money you need to get your solution out into the world. It's best to design a Funding Strategy into your project from the start, though having a great design project can help you raise money along the way. Get any key funding partners together with your design team and Brainstorm (p. 94) the best ways to get your project started. And remember, your Funding Strategy may be different than your ultimate Sustainable Revenue (p. 152) approach so focus on your short-term financial approach here.

STEPS

TIME
60 minutes

DIFFICULTY
Moderate

WHAT YOU'LL NEED
Pens, Post-its, paper

PARTICIPANTS
Design team, key stakeholders, partners

01 | Sit down with your design team, key stakeholders, and partners and start with a Brainstorm about how you might fund the launch of your idea.

02 | If you need to apply for grants or raise money, determine which relationships you may need to develop to help your chances. Creating a Pitch (p. 149) will be very helpful in raising money.

03 | There are lots of ways to raise money outside of traditional channels. Could a crowdfunding platform like Kickstarter or Indiegogo make sense for your idea?

04 | If you're planning to pay for everything by selling a product or service, how many will you need to produce beforehand? If your product or service is free, how does that play into your Funding Strategy?

05 | As you plan your Funding Strategy, also look into the near future. When will you need to break even? How do you bridge from your initial strategy to a long-term Sustainable Revenue plan?

Pilot

A Pilot is a longer-term test of your solution and a critical step before going to market.

If a Live Prototype (p. 135) is a quick look at how your solution behaves in the marketplace, a Pilot is a sustained engagement. Pilots can last months and will fully expose your solution to market forces. At this point you're not testing an idea—Should my product be green? Do I need a different logo?—you're testing an entire system. Ideally you'll have run a few Live Prototypes before going to Pilot so that some of the kinks are worked out. During a Pilot you'll fully execute on your idea finding out if it truly works the way you envisioned by running it with all the staff, space, and resources necessary.

STEPS

TIME
Months

DIFFICULTY
Hard

WHAT YOU'LL NEED
Everything necessary to run your solution

PARTICIPANTS
Design team, key partners, staff

01 First you'll need to sort out all the logistics of your Pilot. Who will you need to hire, should you rent a space, are your distributors and manufacturers lined up, do you need a permit or anything like that?

02 Before you launch your Pilot, strategize how you can differentiate from your competition, how you get customers in the door, or what kind of messaging you need to succeed? You'll be out in the market and you'll need to plan for those dynamics.

03 You'll be iterating less in Pilot because now is the time to truly test your system. You can of course make necessary improvements, but if you change too many variables it may become harder to know what's working and what isn't.

04 As you run your Pilot you'll want to collect information about how your solution is working. Feedback from the people you're designing for is always crucial, but you'll also want to have business metrics to assess your success.

Define Success

Sit down with your team and map out what success looks like. Setting key milestones will keep you on course and give you something to work toward.

Though you've always been driving toward impact with your project, this is a point in the Implementation phase for you to stop and determine how you'll know if you're getting there. You'll determine important milestones in the life of your solution and come to understand what succeeding looks like. Think about a variety of time horizons. What is success in the next two months, in the next year, in five years? Imagine success in terms of both your organization and the people you're designing for. What does success look like in terms of how you've affected them?

STEPS

TIME
90 minutes

DIFFICULTY
Moderate

WHAT YOU'LL NEED
Pens, Post-its, paper

PARTICIPANTS
Design team

01 | Start by returning to your original design challenge. Use that as a lens to think about what success looks like.

02 | Look at your Roadmap (p. 136) and find key delivery dates and milestones. Hitting those dates might be a good indicator of early success. How can you plan to make sure you stay on target?

03 | Imagine what success would look like from different angles. Maybe breaking even by a certain date makes sense from a business perspective. What about success in terms of your organizational operations? What about the perspective of the community you're looking to serve?

04 | Are there any external measures of success that you need to consider? Are funders or partners going to hold you accountable to certain standards? Plan for those as you Define Success.

05 | You can refine how you want to Define Success as you undertake the Monitor and Evaluate (p. 153) Method. They're related and the one will feed the other.

Keep Iterating

Testing, getting feedback, and iterating will help you get a great solution to market and let you know where to push it when you do.

Iteration is the name of the game in human-centered design, and though your solution is now nearly ready to get out into the world, you need to Keep Iterating. Can you tweak your communication strategy, maybe you'll need to evolve your revenue plan, or perhaps your distribution plan needs a rethink? As soon as you get your solution out into the world, start to notice what could be better and assess how you can make it so. By continuing to iterate, soliciting feedback, and building those learnings back into your solution, you'll get further toward having a huge impact.

STEPS

TIME
Throughout the process

DIFFICULTY
Moderate

WHAT YOU'LL NEED
Feedback from the people you're designing for, prototyping materials

PARTICIPANTS
Design team, key stakeholders, partners

01 Don't lose sight of the iterative approach that you've taken so far. As counterintuitive as it might seem, your solution is never truly finished. Even when you've gone to market you can always improve it.

02 Even if your product, service, or experience is in a good place, think about how you're marketing it, if you have the right talent on staff, if you could deliver your solution more effectively. These are all opportunities to iterate.

03 Rapid Prototyping (p. 119) and Live Prototyping (p. 135) are great opportunities to iterate on the fly and quickly test your ideas.

Create a Pitch

Now that your idea is pretty well set, you'll want to communicate it to funders, partners, consumers, everyone!

A pitch is a great way to communicate your idea, how it works, why it counts, and who it benefits. And in the process of making it, you'll clarify the key elements of your idea and refine how you talk about them. A pitch is one of the primary ways that you'll present your idea, and you'll be using it to convince different types of people—from banks to potential customers—to rally to your cause.

STEPS

TIME
90-120 minutes

DIFFICULTY
Moderate

WHAT YOU'LL NEED
Pens, Post-its, Create a Pitch
worksheet p. 185

PARTICIPANTS
Design team

01 | The first thing you'll want to articulate is the essence of your product, service, or experience. Offer context, the main thrust of your idea, why it's different, and any call to action you're making. Try to succinctly explain it in less than a minute.

02 | You'll want your pitch to be clear and unambiguous, so don't get bogged down in the details. Sell your idea by sharing how and why it counts.

03 | Next you'll want to get that story into some kind of format. It could be a pamphlet, a website, a book, or a presentation. You may need more than one. You may need a graphic designer, videographer, or writer to help.

04 | You'll likely communicate differently with different audiences. Make sure that as you Create a Pitch you think about telling stories of varying lengths and in varying degrees of detail. What are the short, medium, and long versions of your pitch?

METHOD IN ACTION

Create a Pitch

The IDEO.org team that worked with the American Refugee Committee (ARC) to create the social business Asili knew that part of bringing the clinic, water point, and agricultural center to life was raising more money. Because our team designed not just the experience, but the service and business model too, they understood how much money ARC needed to raise. And they designed a solution to help get them there.

The pitch that the team created for ARC was two-fold: a video and an operation manual.

"We designed the pitch so that the ARC leadership could go into meetings and show the short video and then walk through a deck that got into more detail," says business designer Shalu Umapathy. "The video served to share the vision, and then the manual was a more granular look at the components of the business and how they work."

One of the trickiest parts of Creating a Pitch is that sometimes the thing your pitching doesn't exist yet. In the case of Asili, the team had to give ARC the tools it needed to sell the service without actually showing it in action.

"It took a ton of planning to do this video," says Umapathy. "Presenting a forward-looking vision of the service was really hard when we couldn't show every part of it. So we figured out how to

make it look like Asili was in place, find props, and community members who would act things out for us while still staying true to the offering. In the end, it worked and the video has been a really useful tool as the ARC leadership team has raised funds for Asili."

When you Create a Pitch, think hard about what you'll need and how to modulate your pitch to different constituencies. And remember that making your pitch catchy, exciting, or urgent can further make the case for your project. Your pitch may even need a couple components, like Asili's video (the vision) and presentation (the details).

Create a Pitch

Succinctly, what is your project?

Asili is a sustainable social business designed to reduce under-five mortality in the Democratic Republic of the Congo. It offers clean water, a health clinic, and agricultural services.

Who do you need to pitch?

Funders

What format(s) will your pitch take?

A video to convey the vision

A presentation that we can make to possible funders

What's your short pitch? As you write it, think about how you'll expand it into a longer one.

In the Democratic Republic of the Congo, 20% of children don't live to see their fifth birthdays. Asili, a new sustainable social enterprise from the American Refugee Committee and IDEO.org, is changing all that. By designing a holistic new approach to health care, food, clean water, and agriculture with the people of the DRC themselves, Asili is ensuring that more kids than ever get the right start.

Sustainable Revenue

Your Funding Strategy will get you through launch, but you'll need a long term revenue strategy to have maximum impact.

There are many kinds of revenue strategies you might use to fund your solution, just be sure that you've got the right one. You've been thinking about revenue throughout your project as you put together your Business Model Canvas (p. 123) and your Funding Strategy (p. 145), but this is another moment to sit down with your design team and key partners and assess if your thinking needs an update. Here, you'll want to answer some critical questions that will affect how you deliver your idea to the people you're designing for.

STEPS

TIME
60 minutes

DIFFICULTY
Moderate

WHAT YOU'LL NEED
Pens, Post-its, paper, spreadsheet

PARTICIPANTS
Design team, key stakeholders, partners

01 Get your design team together with other key stakeholders and partners. Ideally, these same people will have worked on your Funding Strategy and already understand the key elements of your project.

02 Build a simple spreadsheet that shows all of the costs that the solution would incur, from staff to marketing and production.

03 If you're relying on grants or donations, think critically about how you'll raise money and how reliable your funding sources are. What kind of relationships might you need to build to ensure your venture?

04 If you're selling a product, how much of it do you need to sell to hit your revenue goals? How can you keep customers coming back? How much should your product cost? Will you need to introduce new products over time?

05 Finally, as you have all these discussions, think about scaling your project. In five years, will you be operating in more than one location? Will you have multiple products? Is this first offer part of a family of potential goods or services? How can you grow your long-term revenue plans alongside your solution?

Monitor and Evaluate

Your goal has always been to have big impact. Design the ways that you'll measure and grow it into your solution.

Throughout the design process you've constantly been learning, evaluating, and improving your solution. And now that you're on the verge of getting it out into the world you'll need a plan to find out if you're having the impact that you want. There are lots of ways to run a Monitoring and Evaluation (M&E) assessment, the key is to understand what kind is right for you. Sometimes it's easy, either your solution makes money or it doesn't. But if you're trying to change a community's behavior or increase the adoption of a service, you may need a more nuanced approach.

STEPS

TIME
30 minutes

DIFFICULTY
Moderate

WHAT YOU'LL NEED
Pens, Post-its, a wall or board

PARTICIPANTS
Design team

01 | The first thing you'll want to determine is why you need to Monitor and Evaluate your work? Is it to demonstrate impact, to get more funding, to improve business practices, to generate more revenue?

02 | Be sure to bring key partners and stakeholders into this conversation. They may have been Monitoring and Evaluating your topic area for years and can provide key insight.

03 | Assess whether your team is the best suited to Monitor and Evaluate your work. You may need to hire an outside team or consultants to help you.

04 | A common method for assessing impact is a randomized controlled trial (RCT). They are highly rigorous, but are also very expensive and can take years. You'll also be limited in iterating on your solution during an RCT because it may disrupt the test. Dynamic measurement tools (like number of visits or sales numbers) may be more useful for you.

05 | Try to find a balance between quantitative and qualitative measurements. A mix of stories and data can be very powerful.

06 | Take a prototyping attitude to your measurement. You can always tweak your business model based on the information coming in to maximize your impact.

Monitor and Evaluate

In keeping with the human-centered design process as a whole, the Monitoring and Evaluation (M&E) process is rooted in hearing from the community you've designed for and evaluating that feedback to learn what kind of impact you're having. Though your particular sort of evaluation will differ depending on your solution, here is a good place to start to understand what M&E might entail.

Stories and anecdotes are a great first place to ground your measurement. Keeping in mind the context in which you're working and the people you talked to during the Inspiration phase, you can use what you've learned so far to establish a baseline for the current state of the community you're serving. Then get back out there and talk to the community as you implement your solution. This will ensure that you and your team are always grounded in the needs of the people you're designing for, and it will give you a chance to keep learning, iterating, and collecting anecdotes from the community to track against the baseline.

Tracking progress quantitatively through specific indicators can be a powerful complement to the qualitative measurement you've started with. Remember, not every number or data point will be crucial. What's most important is that you have a well-defined goal of what data to gather and how you plan to interpret it. Bear in mind that there are lots of ways to evaluate data, so have a gameplan for which metrics count most when demonstrating your impact.

By rigorously collecting anecdotal feedback and tracking qualitative indicators, you'll be able to more accurately understand the outcomes of your work. Compare these outcomes to the baseline you established at the outset and to your team's goals to assess if you're having the impact you're aiming for.

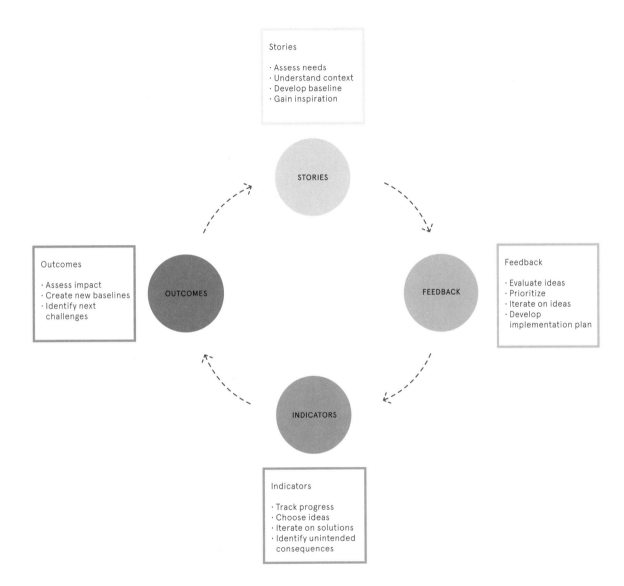

Stories

· Assess needs
· Understand context
· Develop baseline
· Gain inspiration

STORIES

Feedback

· Evaluate ideas
· Prioritize
· Iterate on ideas
· Develop
  implementation plan

FEEDBACK

Outcomes

· Assess impact
· Create new baselines
· Identify next
  challenges

OUTCOMES

Indicators

· Track progress
· Choose ideas
· Iterate on solutions
· Identify unintended
  consequences

INDICATORS

Going to Market

An IDEO.org team working with Marie Stopes International (MSI) and Hewlett Foundation on how to empower teens to take control of their reproductive health arrived at a truly novel solution—a pop-up nail salon where teenage girls can get contraception information and services. But to truly expose the nascent service to market forces, to test it in real-world conditions, they needed to run a live prototype.

Because we're always testing our solutions with the communities we're looking to serve, this live prototype was the perfect opportunity to test three elements in particular: the communication, the outreach, and the physical space.

The communication consisted of the Divine Divas, five fictional archetypes who represent five different methods of birth control. Not only would the Diva characters be put to the test to learn if they had broad appeal to teens, but more importantly, the team would see if the Divas could then spark the kinds of conversations that MSI staff and nurses wanted to have with local teens. Could leading with an aspiration instead of a treatment lead to better outcomes?

Though we got great results with the pop-up nail salon, we needed to learn if it could generate more than short-term interest. And because we learned that teens routinely got questionable information from schools, churches, and their parents, we also wanted to test whether a series of teen connectors—trained, college-aged women who can approach teens on a peer level—would work.

Finally, a redesign of the clinic space itself—where historically girls had been reluctant to get services—was also a major concern. The team took a teen-centric approach by outfitting part of an MSI clinic in bright colors and posting signage with the Divine Divas. Could a more approachable physical space lead to more information and services provided?

With these three questions in mind, MSI ran a three-month live prototype and in that time nearly a thousand girls came for services and treatment. It's a vast increase over MSI's typical numbers, and now, thanks to an extended run in the market, we are confident that our approach has legs. And so is MSI.

Keep Getting Feedback

Even though your idea is now as close to market as it's ever been, you still need the input of the people you're designing for.

Gathering feedback from the people you're designing for is a never-ending process and is critical as you push your idea forward. As you run Live Prototypes (p. 135), Pilot (p. 146) your idea, and determine how to Define Success (p. 147) and Monitor and Evaluate (p. 153) your work, you'll want to have team members dedicated to getting feedback from key partners and the people you're looking to serve.

STEPS

TIME
90 minutes

DIFFICULTY
Moderate

WHAT YOU'LL NEED
Pens, Post-its, notebook

PARTICIPANTS
Design team, people you're designing for, key stakeholders, partners

01 As you move into Live Prototyping and Pilot, make sure that you're collecting feedback. Interviews (p. 39) and Group Interviews (p. 42) are a great way to learn from the people you're designing for.

02 Reach out to key partners as well for their input. They'll often have expertise that the design team may not and can help point the way forward. Convening the right group of stakeholders all at once can bring up a lot of feedback in a single session.

03 Capture feedback in your notebook and share back with the design team. You can do this by Sharing Inspiring Stories (p. 78) and Downloading Your Learnings (p. 77).

—

Case Study: Clean Team

In-Home Toilets for Ghana's Urban Poor

For the millions of Ghanaians without in-home toilets, there are few good options when it comes to our bodies' most basic functions. Working with Unilever and Water and Sanitation for the Urban Poor (WSUP), IDEO.org developed Clean Team, a comprehensive sanitation system that delivers and maintains toilets in the homes of subscribers. Clean Team now serves thousands of people in Kumasi, Ghana, making lives cleaner, healthier, and more dignified.

DESIGN TEAM
8 IDEO.org designers

PARTNERS
Water and Sanitation for the Urban
Poor (WSUP), Unilever

TIMELINE
20 weeks

LOCATION
Kumasi and Accra, Ghana

THE OUTCOME

An IDEO.org team designed a comprehensive sanitation system to serve the needs of low-income Ghanaians. The Clean Team service is a custom-designed stand-alone rental toilet as well as a waste-removal system, but the design work extended to the entire service ecosystem including branding, uniforms, a payment model, a business plan, and key messaging. Unilever and WSUP piloted the project with about 100 families in the city of Kumasi, Ghana, before launching in 2012.

INSPIRATION

The Inspiration phase of the project was intense, with scores of interviews needed to understand all facets of the design challenge. "Because sanitation is a systems-level challenge we knew that we couldn't just design Clean Team's toilet," says team member and designer Danny Alexander.

After six weeks of talking with sanitation experts, shadowing a toilet operator, digging into the history of sanitation in Ghana, and talking to scads of Ghanaians, key insights about what the toilet should look like and how waste should be collected emerged.

An important historical note came out too: For years Ghana had night soil collectors, people who cleaned out bucket latrines each night. But because many night soil collectors dumped human waste in the streets, night soil collection was banned in the 1990s as a threat to public health. This meant the team could leverage an existing behavior around in-home waste removal, but they would have to avoid any association with illegal dumping.

IDEATION

This was a lightning-fast phase in the project, one that leapt from learnings to prototypes in seven weeks. After brainstorming with its partners and everyday Ghanaians, the team determined which direction to take and began testing its ideas. What aesthetics did people like? Would a urine-diverting toilet work? Would people allow servicemen into their homes? Where in the home would the toilet go? Can you design a toilet that can only be emptied at a waste management facility?

By building a handful of prototypes and modifying existing portable toilets, the team got tangible elements of the service into the hands of Ghanaians. They learned how the service should be positioned, early ideas around marketing and promotion, as well as certain technical limitations, namely that though flush functions appeared popular early in the goings, water scarcity was a major factor to contend with and nobody relishes disposing of his own waste.

IMPLEMENTATION

Once the service offerings and look and feel of the toilet were more or less fleshed out, WSUP ran a live prototype of the Clean Team service. Because tooling for toilet manufacture is so expensive, WSUP used off-the-shelf cabin toilets, which approximated about 80% of the toilets that IDEO.org would design, to test the service. They got great results, went ahead with manufacturing, and as of 2012, the toilets were in production. They sport IDEO.org-created branding and the Clean Team service has found its way into the lives of thousands of people.

Frame Your Design Challenge

What is the problem you're trying to solve?

1) **Take a stab at framing it as a design question.**

2) **Now state the ultimate impact you're trying to have.**

3) **What are some possible solutions to your problem?**
Think broadly. It's fine to start a project with a hunch or two, but make sure you allow for surprising outcomes.

4) **Finally, write down some of the context and constraints that you're facing.**
They could be geographic, technological, time-based, or have to do with the population you're trying to reach.

5) **Does your original question need a tweak? Try it again.**

Interview Guide

Open General

What are some broad questions you can ask to open the conversation and warm people up?

Then Go Deep

What are some questions that can help you start to understand this person's hopes, fears, and ambitions?

Resource Flow

For individual interviews:

What brings money in?   Where does money go?

For Group Interviews:

What brings money in?   Where does money go?

Card Sort

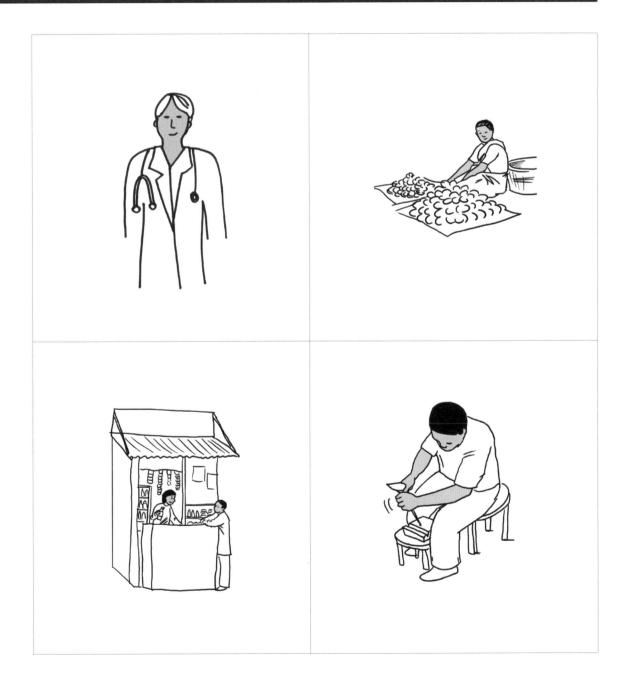

Card Sort

Card Sort

Card Sort

Create Insight Statements

Write Your Design Challenge

Theme: ....

Insights:

1.

2.

3.

Theme: ....

Insights:

1.

2.

3.

Theme: ....

Insights:

1.

2.

3.

Create How Might We Questions

Turn Your Insights Into How Might We Questions

Insight:

_____

How might we _____

Insight:

_____

How might we _____

Insight:

_____

How might we _____

Storyboard

Title

Place Post-It
Drawing Here

What's Happening

Title

Place Post-It
Drawing Here

What's Happening

Title

Place Post-It
Drawing Here

What's Happening

Title

Place Post-It
Drawing Here

What's Happening

Business Model Canvas

Designed for: Designed by:

Key Partners

Who are our Key Partners? Who are our key suppliers? Which Key Resources are we acquiring from partners? Which Key Activities do partners perform?

Key Activities

What Key Activities do our value propostions require? Our distribution Channels? Revenue Streams?

Key Resources

What Key Resources do our value propositions require? Our distribution Channels? Customer Relationships? Revenue Streams?

Key Propositions

What value do we deliver to the customer? Which one of our customer's problems are we helping to solve? What bundles of products and services are we offering to each Customer Segment? Which customer needs are we satisfying?

Cost Structure

What are the most important costs inherent in our business model? Which Key Resources are most expensive? Which Key Activities are most expensive?

Date: Version:

Customer Relationships

What type of relationship does each of our Customer Segments expect us to establish and maintain with them? Which ones have we established? How are they integrated with the rest of our business model? How costly are they?

Customer Segments

For whom are we creating value?
Who are our most important customers?

Channels

Through which Channels do our Customer Segments want to be reached? How are we reaching them now? How are our Channels integrated? Which ones work best? Which ones are most cost-efficient? How are we integrating them with customer routines?

Revenue Streams

For what value are our customers really willing to pay?
For what do they currently pay? How are they currently paying? How would they prefer to pay? How much does each Revenue Stream contribute to overall revenues?

Strategyzer
strategyzer.com

Resource Assessment

Distribution	Activities	Capabilities
How are you getting your concept out into the world? Are there multiple ways?	What activities will be required to make your idea work?	What are we already capable of?

	Responsibilities				Still Needed?
	Who is responsible for doing it?				
	Design Team	Implementing Org	Funder	External	

Ways to Grow Framework

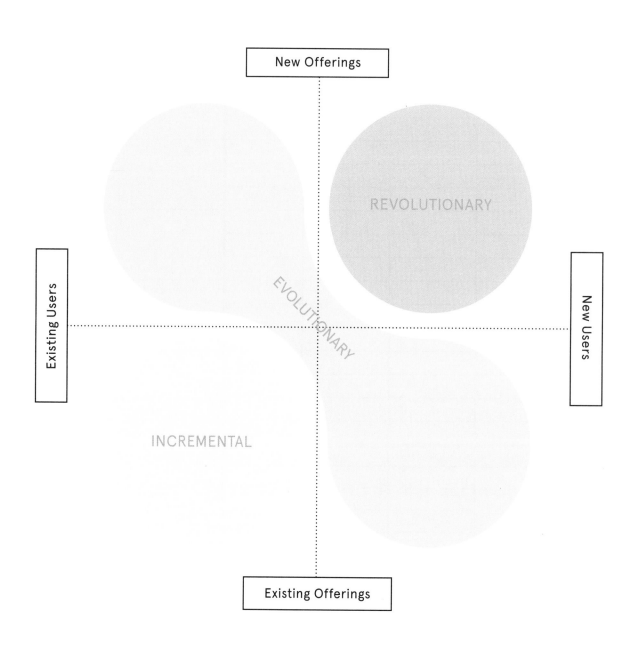

New Offerings

Existing Users

REVOLUTIONARY

EVOLUTIONARY

New Users

INCREMENTAL

Existing Offerings

Create a Pitch

Succinctly, what is your project?

Who do you need to pitch?

What format(s) will your pitch take?

What's your short pitch? As you write it, think about how you'll expand it into a larger one.

NOTES

brought to you by

IDEO·ORG

The Field Guide to Human-Centered Design was designed and written by IDEO.org in San Francisco. It's an evolution of the Human-Centered Design Toolkit, a book originally produced by IDEO in 2011. Years on from the HCD Toolkit's first publication, we've learned so much about how to use design to combat poverty, and the Field Guide is a chance to share what we've picked up along the way in the hope that you can put it into practice too.

We'd like to thank our 1300+ supporters on Kickstarter who made the Field Guide possible. We couldn't have done it without our community of designers, entrepreneurs, and social sector innovators, the very people we believe will use the Field Guide to help change the world.

For more on human-centered design, visit **designkit.org.**

To learn more about our work, check out **ideo.org.**